Winning

in

2025

Also by Michael de Kare-Silver:

Digital Insights 2020
e-Shock
Strategy in Crisis
Stre@mlining
Building the 2020 Digital Team

Winning

in

2025

Digital and Data Transformation:
The Keys to Success

Michael de Kare-Silver

Matador
9 Priory Business Park,
Wistow Road, Kibworth Beauchamp,
Leicestershire. LE8 0RX
Tel: 0116 279 2299
Email: books@troubador.co.uk
Web: www.troubador.co.uk/matador
Twitter: @matadorbooks

ISBN 978 1789018 066

British Library Cataloguing in Publication Data.
A catalogue record for this book is available from the British Library.

Printed and bound by CPI Group (UK) Ltd, Croydon, CR0 4YY
Typeset in 11pt Aldine401 BT by Troubador Publishing Ltd, Leicester, UK

Matador is an imprint of Troubador Publishing Ltd

This is dedicated to Deborah and Alexander
– best friends, muse and inspiration

Contents

Chapter 1

Winning in 2025

Leading organisations today are asking: what's it take to be a winner in 2025? If we were to build our company from scratch in today's digital technology world, then what would that look like? What new products / services might we have, what new partnerships and alliances might we form, what kind of digital eco-system would we establish, what new investments, stake-holdings, even acquisitions, what would our "Business 2025" look like?

To drive towards this, most every company nowadays is on a journey, a journey to transform, to change, to take advantage of new technologies, new innovations new ideas. Some of that work is focussed on costs and efficiency, and that's especially true in B2B and in Manufacturing. However, a lot of the work is also focussed on future growth, finding new revenue streams, new options for business and development, new ways to engage with customers, new techniques to drive customer immersion and conversion. It's all about how to rewire the business, how to establish the future operating model, how best to organise, where to focus investment and resources, how to build the talent pool with the right skills and know-how, how to motivate employees and the entire workforce for this new digital age.

IDC Research and Forbes estimate that c. $1 trillion is being invested annually by corporations globally on technologies and services that will enable digital and data transformation. IDC comments that: "some of the strategic priority areas include building cognitive /AI capabilities, data-driven services and benefits, operationalizing data and information, digital trust and stewardship and omni-channel customer engagement". In a Gartner survey, "94% of executives- in other words, just about everyone – say they have increased focus on digital growth, and 90 percent say digital plays a central role in their overarching business goals. Everyone is being told to go digital, and the reaction is to throw ever-growing amounts of money at technology solutions." On average most multi-national corporations of scale will have at least two major technology-led transformation programmes taking place in each department and in each country /business unit. There's a lot going on!

This activity is fuelled by the rapid advancements in Tech which challenge existing business models and suggest new futures. Retail is an obvious example now in which the shift to online and e-commerce has meant large scale physical bricks 'n mortar estates may no longer be viable or necessary. Retailers are now rushing to close stores and shift to the new multi-channel model. And this kind of seismic shift is happening in many B2C /consumer-facing businesses. Traditional channels and means of communication are no longer the business drivers and key levers they used to be. So how to adapt, how change, how reinvent, how do this quickly, how do this quickly while maintaining levels of sales and profitability, how do this at a pace that will maintain or increase shareholder value and not allow a substantial collapse in market value, how make sure that the investments in digital and data technology are the optimal ones that do deliver the targeted value and RoI?

It's not just a micro-company challenge. There are also macro forces at work as countries vie for economic advantage and success and look to advance their infrastructure and networks that will enable private enterprise to succeed. China is at the forefront of channelling investment into key areas and looking to build global market leadership. Xi Jinping, as President of China, announced that: "Supremacy in AI is a core strategic goal and we have directed plans to dominate global AI by 2030". China has also made bold statements around "Made in China 2025" which will focus investment to upgrade core manufacturing sectors such as Robotics, Aerospace and Energy-saving vehicles. This investment program in China will channel significant government subsidies, government-sponsored (paid-for) R&D and setting targets for local manufacturing content.

Japan is another country proactively stimulating and encouraging investment in targeted key industries. Announcements have been made by Shinzo Abe as Prime Minister about focussed investment in Life Sciences, ICT (Information and Communications Technology), Sensor Technology and Nano Technology. "We are looking to take full advantage of advances in genome and biology research, wearable devices (eg smart contact lenses), and "big data" insights driving advances in medical care and we aim to reinvigorate the contribution from manufacturing to our GDP as we advance towards 2025."

As exciting as it is to read of all this activity and investment and tech-led opportunity, it's also a worrying time for people at work. There are many headlines about how robotics and automation will replace people, how there will be fewer jobs and how the types of jobs available and skills needed are changing. That might perhaps be of less concern to a young millennial embarking on their first career and able to hopefully develop the future skills required. But these sort of technology changes are less helpful for someone in mid-career who may have to retrain in order to secure future employment. It's a very difficult area and in an economic environment which boasts lower unemployment in a number of developed economies and hard to find and recruit people, those forecasts of robots doing all the work seem far way, almost science fiction still. Except that competitive forces will compel companies to examine these opportunities and may often be required to change just to survive.

It's hard to predict the future of course but what we do know, as Bill Gates has so aptly put it, is "that we tend to overestimate the short term but underestimate the long term". Forecasters will often talk about immediate impact but in practice things do take longer to unfold. What does happen, is that when for example innovation reaches some kind of critical mass, then its development can be exponential. The oft-cited example is the smart phone, launched in 2007 and in ten years, global and ubiquitous.

For companies today, the challenge is immense, how navigate through this fast-changing world, how anticipate what to invest in, what new tech to embrace, what future operating model to adopt, what sort of competitive landscape to face in 2025 and how succeed, how find those sources of competitive advantage which will ensure the company becomes /stays a winner? As companies face up to these challenges and opportunities, they are reminded just how many transformations do fail, just how difficult it is to make this navigation successfully. McKinsey research shows that c. 70% of digital transformation programmes fail. Cognizant research showed that 53% of execs interviewed felt that their company was not ready or able to digest and take advantage of new tech investment and change. Only 26% of people in research by BARC felt their company was taking advantage of the data they had available. In GE, at one point there were over 200 major transformation programmes going on with an estimated near $500m technology investment behind them. Most every function and country had embarked on its own change initiatives, significant amounts were being spent on consultancy and contractor support, there was so much going on there that very little was being effectively implemented, projects were not joined-up, resources were over-stretched and BAU (business as usual) activity was being side-lined given the focus on delivering change. As one exec there put it: "we were in chaos". While GE is now coming through that period with a new focus, the company in the meantime, is struggling to still be a winner.

This book then examines these challenges and opportunities. It looks at what does a company need to do now, today, to make the right decisions for tomorrow. It considers the keys to drive transformation successfully, ways to most effectively engage employees and all the workforce, how best to organise and structure to unleash the energies and empower employees to own and embrace change. It's not an easy journey, but there are many case studies described in this book that will show the pitfalls to avoid and the better practice steps to take.

Chapter 2

Digital + Data: the twin imperatives

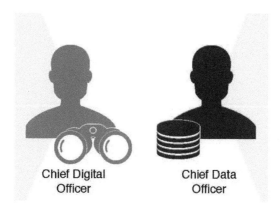

Chief Digital
Officer

Chief Data
Officer

First, let's consider some core stats and headlines:

"Whoever becomes the leader in Data and Artificial Intelligence will rule the world"

-President Vladimir Putin

"China has made supremacy in AI a strategic goal and has announced plans to dominate global AI by 2030"

-Financial Times

"The internet economy in China is forecast to be more than US$1 trillion in 2020"

-Center for Retail Research

"Amazon.com revenues are close to US$ 250bn and 40% of all US e-commerce"

-USA Today

"In China, e-commerce is reaching towards 25% of all retail sales, in the UK it's getting close to 20%, South Korea is at 16%, USA at 15% and Denmark at 12%"

-Statista

"5 billion videos each day are watched on YouTube"

-BrandWatch

"More data was created in the two years 2017 and 2018 than in the previous 5,000 years of humanity"

-Forbes

"Annual data creation today is approximately 16 Zettabytes (that's 16 trillion gigabytes or 16,000 exabytes), by 2025 that is expected to increase 10-fold"

-IDC Survey

"We live in a world where we now take for granted immediate global connectivity, immediate interaction and response and we accept no limits on availability, service and supply"

-Marc Andreessen

"Data is expanding across every industry from biotech, healthcare and pharma through to all forms of social media and entertainment and the emerging "internet of things" will be a new tipping point"

-PA Consulting

Data and Digital have now become the twin imperatives most impacting companies. Research is suggesting that the winners in 2025 will be those who best master them both.

We have all been acutely aware of how Digital generally is transforming the way companies do business and how customers prefer to interact and purchase. Now, Data has come to the fore and whether it's Machine Learning or AI or real time predictive analytics, companies are facing major competitive pressures to gain new insight into the ways they operate and engage with customers and drive new sources of advantage.

This chapter looks at these key pressures, examines best practices and how some companies are managing to respond successfully and learning how best to move forward and be one of those next decade winners.

★★★★★

The consulting firm BCG has described the new Digital + Data dynamic as "a question of life or death in most industries". In their most recent survey, BCG found that 72% of senior company execs felt that successfully mastering these two challenges would be the key to their survival. Most talked about significant change and transformation programmes under way. Most acknowledged that there were substantial market share and profit gains to be had if they could better their competitors in these areas. Most were spending increasing amounts of time and investment $ on transformation processes, structures, technology infrastructure, ways of working, company culture, skills training etc. But, most also said that they had yet to see the results coming through, that it was taking much longer than they thought, that they worried new disruptors would emerge who could undermine their business model, that perhaps some of the investment was not being channelled or deployed or implemented in the right way, and that it was leading to growing frustrations in the ranks.

Most also looked at what had already happened in Publishing, Music, Consumer Electricals, Education, Stock trading, Travel, Payment systems, small component Manufacturing (through 3D printing); they envied how quickly the likes of Uber or Airbnb, or SimplyBusiness or DirectAsia or challenger banks (eg Aldemore, Monzo) or others had arrived on the scene and totally changed the industry dynamic, levels of profitability and future opportunities. Most worried about: *how can we pull off our own transformation?*

What's clear is that the next decade winners will be the digital and data transformation masters. We can just see that from this chart below; how the

Data-Driven Companies Have Become the Most Valuable

Rank	2018	Q4 2011	Q4 2006
	Company: Market Capitalization ($billions)		
1	Apple: 1,000	Exxon Mobil: 406	Exxon Mobil: 447
2	Alphabet: 800	Apple: 376	General Electric: 384
3	Microsoft: 800	PetroChina: 277	Microsoft: 294
4	Amazon: 860	Royal Dutch Shell: 237	Citigroup: 274
5	Facebook: 440	ICBC: 228	Gazprom: 271
6	Berkshire Hathaway: 545	Microsoft: 218	ICBC: 255
7	Exxon Mobil: 545	IBM: 217	Toyota: 241
8	Johnson & Johnson: 380	Chevron: 212	Bank of America: 240
9	JPMorgan Chase: 370	Walmart: 205	Royal Dutch Shell: 223
10	Alibaba Group: 400	China Mobile: 196	BP: 219

Data-Driven Company

[Source: S&P Capital IQ, "Top 10 Companies with Highest Market Capitalization Worldwide." Note: Market capitalization figures have been rounded and are in $billions.

most valuable companies of today are now typically those regarded as digital and data leaders and while market cap will fluctuate, the overall dominance of these sort of corporations is compelling.

What emerges from the research into best practice is the need for the whole organisation to buy into this wholesale transformation need. If there is a burning platform, for example as we can see among high street retailers, then the drive, the energy, the need for change can act as a tremendous catalyst. Where there is no such urgency, then it does require a significant communications exercise to engage the whole workforce on this journey.

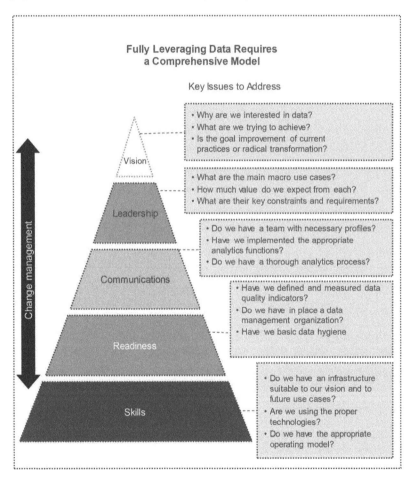

In another survey, this time by Altimeter, they also found that the majority of companies reported they are undergoing some form of digital and or data-led transformation. 85% of that group said they had a time frame of less that 3 years to make a success of that or suffer financially. But, only 25% of the surveyed companies felt they had a clear understanding of what the path to success would be.

Against this backcloth, with companies clearly identifying the need for change, what then is the biggest hurdle to success. What is the key ingredient that can make the difference, that can turn that 25% stat into 100%?

A recent survey from Forrester suggests that a key factor is "talent and leadership". And a new report from MIT/Cap Gemini concluded that 87% of companies *"have a critical skills shortage in digital and data transformation".* Have we got the right people in the right place with the drive and energy and talent to drive through these changes? Do we have a CEO who sees this as their No. 1 priority? For example, at Aviva, the successful insurance group, it's said that the Leadership Exec there set up Digital teams to deliberately challenge and game-change the core business, be a competitor to it, establish the "digital first" model as the preferred way for customers to interact and in effect make the traditional business model redundant. Who else has that bravery, that willingness to challenge and change all the formerly established ways of doing business?

At Bupa, another insurer, they are just at the beginning of their true digital transformation. And one potentially highly successful initiative is their Customer Lab. Set up at the Group Centre, its remit is to define and design the Bupa digital and data business model of the future. To take certain core parts of the business and do a stand-alone rebuild as if they were starting from scratch, as a pure play, and to leave behind all legacy and hierarchy and traditional process and ways of working. This "Customer Lab" is centre stage at Bupa, reports direct to the CEO and has the mandate to rebuild the company.

Finding the key talent to lead the digital and data transformation is not easy, but in the "war for talent" there is in fact a strong talent pool who do have the necessary skills. Research from Gartner identified the 5 key attributes of successful transformation leaders:

(i) *Exceptional stakeholder management skills.*
(ii) *Ability to listen*
(iii) *Technical knowledge (though not necessarily a Techie!)*
(iv) *Stature, maturity, years of experience*
(v) *Have the clear CEO and Board mandate and authority to act and make decisions*

Gartner found that in 64% of companies surveyed, the transformation leaders did not meet these criteria. In more than 80% of situations there was no dedicated transformation person in that role on the Board or ExCo, and frequently that key change leadership role was "buried" in the hierarchy and often had no real power or authority to change.

If that's the case then perhaps no wonder there is so much frustration and disappointment around the change agenda.

Let's look at some companies who are bucking the trend and getting it right.

Adobe has developed a track record for consistent annual profits and earnings growth and often at double digit levels. Adobe CEO Shantanu Narayen commented: "Our strong business momentum is driven by the market-leading solutions we provide to empower people to create and businesses to digitally transform and *by our own continued digital and data transformation*"

Adobe has evolved from a traditional desktop software provider of multi-media products to now a Cloud-based services provider, changing its business model to a subscription-base and a focus on digital design and data analytics. Shantanu Narayen has been very much the driver of the Adobe business transformation. He is well-known for stopping people in the corridor and asking *what working on /what have you contributed today to our transformation agenda*, focus on that priority and not on other things. That has sent a clear message to everyone about what is critical. In addition, there have been monthly all-company updates on progress and quarterly group "town hall" meetings to update and share best practices.

Alongside the very personal and direct involvement of the CEO, it's been made clear that this is the No. 1 priority of the management team. There has been some restructuring of the senior leadership, a new dedicated Transformation / Change team put in place reporting direct to the ExCo and substantial across-the-company training programs to upskill in change management and to reinforce the value of what's been targeted.

"Developing a "digital first" mindset has been key for us, we are modernising the way we develop our software and the applications and tools around that. It enables us to reduce productions costs, speed time to market and move services across different cloud platforms. Also, because we now have real time data insights on customer usage we can evolve and introduce new features fast. We can now better monetise our assets and customer services".

As the Adobe CEO said: *"if we don't reinvent, then someone will reinvent us out of business".*

Some other snapshot examples: *Sprint* is looking to its future success on the back of building a true data leadership capability versus the likes of Verizon and AT&T, and this led by CIO Scott Rice: "we are redesigning the whole customer journey experience based on our new understanding of the data…and this data transformation, based around Agile methods of working, is now reaching out across all aspects of the business". *StubHub* is looking at a total redesign of its data and technology platform, moving to Cloud-based solutions that can handle the huge amounts of data and "can scale elastically…it's required a major upgrade of our change leadership group". *Target*, the US retailer, is another undergoing a major transformation, with ex Tesco CIO Mike McNamara to build a new tech and digital capability team. Retailer *Best Buy* has brought in new Chief Digital Officer Brian Tilzer to work alongside CMO Barry Judge to drive digital transformation and establishing a core digital innovation lab to be at the heart of all future product /service development. Others like UPS, ING Bank, Saint Gobain, Aviva, Elsevier, SAP, Syngenta…these are all emerging as leaders in their sectors with a transformation momentum and culture which is ongoing and establishing a strong platform for future success.

★★★★★

Achieving this transformation success is not easy. GE, as already referred to, has for example been on a long and much-discussed transformation journey but has struggled to deliver the breakthroughs and targets it had planned. The company has worked tirelessly to train its workforce in a "digital first" mindset but has also been struggling with shifts in its core energy division where technology has rapidly changed what customers are looking for. In addition, it is grappling with a huge and globally distributed workforce of more than 300,000 and operates across a wide number of industry sectors from aviation to financial services to healthcare. It seems like the further away the workforce are from GE HQ now in Boston, the harder it has been to instil that change mindset.

Nevertheless GE insiders remain optimistic. "We are still among the largest global companies in terms of revenues (>$120bn and 13th largest on the Fortune 500). Yes, we started the change journey some years ago but we are even now transformed from a traditional industrial company. Industry 4.0 with all its focus on digital and process automation and supply chain connectivity is something we wholeheartedly embrace". A new CEO Lawrence Culp arrived with a remit to turbo charge the transformation process, all the 300,000 workforce have been retrained, again, the GE Global Research Center is now an innovation hotbed trialling new revenue streams leveraging eg blockchain technology and advanced robotics, there's been a new announced partnership with Apple to develop apps together, there's a big push to embrace Cloud-based solutions enabling GE to close most of its own data centres, it has embraced product internet connectivity and IoT, the "internet of things", eg equipping its MRI scanners with sensors to develop a digital trail of data on machine performance and remote monitoring…it's looking more and more to become software and data analytics-led. That's a wrenching change of company culture, investment and priority and some commentators are now pushing for splitting up the company and its major divisions, demerge parts and give them perhaps more freedom to develop the necessary agile change mindset. And at the time of writing, GE had sold off its Commercial Lighting, Aircraft Systems and Power Conversion businesses, with more business unit sell-offs being discussed.

The jury is out on whether GE will succeed but they do offer a very good illustration and example of a company that recognises the need for change, brings in new leadership, changes its senior team, and has the desire and ambition led very personally by a well-rated Exec team to engage the whole organisation in its change journey.

Chapter 3

Building an effective Data & Analytics capability

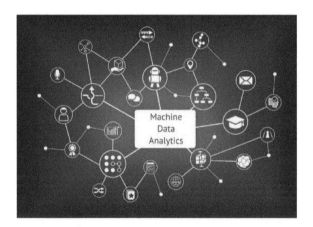

A recent KPMG survey described Data expertise as: "the most in-demand skill for the second year running" with 39% of companies saying they struggled to find the right talent to lead this area. The Harvard Business Review has declared that "data science and analytics is the sexiest job of the century!" Research company Gartner has suggested that there will be as many as 4 million new big data jobs coming up worldwide over the next few years.

Getting insight out of data, driving ideas and innovation that can better target and engage customers, enabling more informed decision-making, helping manage and reduce risk, improving performance, taking advantage of machine learning tools...all these applications of data management, analytics and insight are key areas of opportunity of course in today's data rich world.

But in a recent survey by BARC Research, only 26% of execs interviewed felt that their companies were making effective use of the data they had. That's a significant majority who felt that data was not being fully exploited in their organisation. As a sign of what's missing, or perhaps better said, what the potential could be, 54% of execs in the same survey said that they did hope! to get more involved in using data insights in the future.

There's a massive untapped potential here. Everyone will agree about the "power of data". But it's often the exploitation of that data that is still missing.

The focus on the power of data and analytics has been increased because of developments in data science. Machine Learning and Artificial Intelligence are bringing a whole new wave of ideation and insight and new ways of working and new possible streams of revenue and profitability. It's a massive opportunity and companies have raced to build their data science teams. This is especially true in financial services where companies like Aviva, Barclays, Zurich Insurance and others now often talk about having teams of more than 500 to 1000 data scientists across their international businesses all focussed on next generation opportunities.

This rush to data science has had several consequences. Demand exceeds supply. There just aren't enough data scientists to go round. It means that salaries have increased significantly as companies find they are forced to pay a premium. And it's not uncommon to hear that a Bank or Insurer is in the market with a recruitment goal of hiring eg 25 data scientists in the next 3 months – for just one of their local country operating teams. So even new graduates out of university are finding they are being swept up in this enthusiastic rush. And they are attracted to it as the salaries on offer are high. It also means that many such data teams are relatively junior, maybe only a few years work experience and so lack leaders with deep managerial experience. They may all be good computer scientists and software engineers but their stakeholder management skills, their political nous on how best to operate inside a large corporation, their interpersonal skills and ways of communicating...these sort of necessary team leadership skills are sometimes lacking.

All this has led to a disconnect between Senior Exec /Board level ambitions and expectations versus what is actually happening in the data science team, their output and what they are delivering. The data geeks are busy developing new AI tools and algorithms but all that isn't necessarily translating into new product /service features and solutions that do make an impact in the market *and* deliver the RoI.

So a number of organisations are now adding further to their data science investments by inserting Transformation experts who can review the way data science is organised and "operationalise and systematise" the way things are done, its processes and core interactions so that the substantial potential can be captured and realised. Though there's a need to drive this carefully as too much control can of course extinguish the necessary spirit of innovation and entrepreneurship that can uncover the big new idea that can make the difference.

Companies are learning. They have rushed to adopt these good ideas and now need to find the best ways to make that work. Making it work may need the insertion of "transformation experts" but it might also be about establishing a more effective structure which encourages the broader company-wide adoption of the data science ideas and capabilities.

In many organisations for example, data skill and function areas are set up in an individual business area, operate in silos with their own agendas and reporting lines and so will often only collaborate cross-function /across the company to share ideas if there is a clear mandate and shared view that this is indeed a strategic priority.

Typically data science sits in the IT /Technology group. Historically it is this function who have been the early initiators of projects around data and data warehousing. They have the relationships with the analytical software vendors like Oracle/Siebel or Adobe or SAS or AgilOne or the many smaller alternative suppliers and so will likely be the early advocates and adopters. But as a recent Accenture Interactive survey pointed out: "CIO leadership of data and analytics can work well. But that is provided it is *intertwined* with the other c-Suite leaders and especially the CMO and the customer marketing team. Without very close collaboration, data and analytics can end up being an IT team software project instead of an insight into performance and the voice of the customer".

Recent research from an IBM /Constellation ThinkTank has also highlighted that collaboration around the data science agenda is going to be a key and that a failure to collaborate is a major reason for lack of progress. They advocate that more CMOs and more Marketing departments do now need to step forward. And if not seize control of this area at least make sure that the "intertwining" is happening and working. The research suggests that Marketers are not intuitively comfortable with data and detailed analysis. But with the proliferation of marketing and communication channels, IBM /Constellation emphasise it is imperative for Marketing teams to still be the "voice of the customer" and so have that close insight and understanding to better drive performance insight and more personalised and more cost-effective customer activity.

The challenge then is how to build an effective data and data science team that works, that does effectively cut through the data value chain and deliver the RoI all are expecting. If we look at the skills and jobs required to build this capability then it's clear we are looking at a substantial task of team development and cross-company integration.

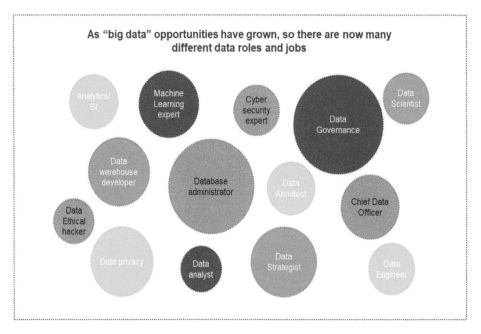

As "big data" opportunities have grown, so there are now many different data roles and jobs

This shows just how many different and specific skills and areas of expertise are required. Companies may often ask to hire eg a "Head of Data" or a Chief Data Officer but when asked what they want that person to do and focus on, then the answer is sometimes vague and indeterminate. Yet, clearly any head of data will need to be able to focus, is the challenge more a software /technology issue or it more for example around the customer analytics? Depending on the answer may well influence the sort of background and skills the "Head of" person should have. Do they need to connect with the IT community most, or with Marketing and Sales, where do the opportunities lie both short term and long term and what required to deliver them?

Assuming there are budgets and scope to build out an effective Data team, then the suggested start-point is to hire in the **Data Strategist**. This person is the one who will build the business case, meet the key stakeholders, identify the potential "size of prize", determine at a top line a possible team and possible investment and so define the possible outcomes and RoI. The person best placed to do that may not even have any data expertise themselves. But they bring an MBA-type, commercial approach, can take a fresh perspective and critically can interact at Board level to determine a strategic plan of action.

Once agreed then there will be a number of key next step appointments needed:

1. The Data Architect

This person will be the designer, they will develop the technical architecture that needs to be developed. They will decide for example on what software platform(s), whether to build in-house or use established software tools and solutions, how much can /should be Cloud-based, who best to partner with.

In many ways this is the most critical hire and appointment as this person is determining the whole future roadmap and blueprint for the organisation. So finding someone who has "been there and done it" and done it successfully is so important.

They also need to have enough credibility and authority that they can win the respect and support especially of the CTO but also the other key business leaders who can accept being guided by this person.

2. Data Analysts

This may be a small team and they are the ones who will feed off the work from the Strategist and the Architect. They will be getting into the detail, understanding the use-case requirements, investigating the areas of opportunity so they can spec out exactly what level of software and functionality and skills are needed.

3. Data Engineers

These are the people who will build-out the overall architecture and design. They may have expertise in enterprise data solutions such as Oracle, IBM or Microsoft or more dedicated niche providers such as Tibco, EnterWorks or RiverSand. They will be building the infrastructure that will enable the data management. They will also be the integrators who will ensure the interoperability of any new solutions with the main operating platform. They will also have responsibility for delivery, testing and maintenance.

4. Data Scientists

The data scientists will be the machine learning /AI experts. They may have PhDs in Maths or Statistics or Computer Sciences. They are excited about building new products /services and applications. They have been described as "the alchemists of the 21st century"! Their core skill is turning raw data into insight and they will want to be hands-on coders as that is what most energises them.

This also highlights the earlier point that as this area scales up so inevitably it will need team leaders and managers who will need to spend more time managing and communicating while perhaps coaching the more junior developers and this interpersonal skill set is in very short supply in this data science arena. Not easy to find PhD data scientists who can interact confidently and effectively with senior Business /Function heads across the organisation and translate the Tech talk into commercial terms which others can understand!

5. Data Governance

In today's world, data management, data privacy, who has access, how data can be used, what processes need to be in place to ensure data is managed… this area needs to be taken care of. And in the Financial Services sector especially there are substantial amounts of regulation and compliance that need to be implemented, monitored and reported on. It is a significant and now high-profile role. It may well be a job taken by a former practising lawyer who has that attention to minute detail and protocol and can manage through the substantial layers of bureaucracy.

6. The CSO

The Chief Security Officer is possibly the least attractive job. This is the person who will get the call at 2am on a Sunday morning if there has been a leak of personal data. This is the person who is most in the spotlight unfortunately if something goes wrong! So those who take the role will likely be obsessive security experts who will be trying to ensure that nothing can go wrong. They will likely employ their own 24/7 "ethical hacking" teams who are constantly testing the systems' defences and identifying any potential leak or lack of adequate security before an outside third party can discover it.

A report from Cisco /IT Governance reported more than 200 major targeted cyber-attacks in the USA in one year which had each impacted more than 1 million personal data records each time. In addition, 31% of companies had experienced some form of hacking. Companies like Uber, Equifax and Under Armour have reported attacks eg affecting, in the case of Equifax, more than 150 million people. And the costs of managing and defending keep going up. Aside from the team needed to manage these situations, companies say that costs have increased by more than 20% and now there are ransom-ware costs, loss of information, potential loss of customers, the adverse publicity…it's estimated that the cost to Equifax was more than $4bn.

The biggest area of potential damage is through email. Simple phishing which encourages an email to be opened, a link clicked can cause untold damage and some 90% of all data breaches come about this way. This is something that companies can try to protect against and one example comes from Nationwide, the UK Bank /Building Society. They have trained all their 18,000 employees in cyber security and have set up a very rigorous system around that. Test emails are periodically sent out to staff to check if they have understood all the training. If an employee nevertheless does click the test link, then they are asked to go to be retrained. If the same person makes the mistake a second time then they are given a formal warning. And a third time has the risk of being asked to leave the company.

This may sound like a tough regime, but it is inevitably the way most companies are headed and will have to set up some sort of similar monitoring programme to heighten awareness around this issue.

That's why the CSO job is probably one of the least popular and at the same time the most onerous!

★★★★★

If all this data team is to work effectively it will naturally need the right leadership and there are three key roles that should be considered:

1. Chief Data Officer
2. Director/VP of Data Science
3. Director/VP of Customer Insight & Analytics

1. Chief Data Officer

Forrester research summed up this crucial leadership role: *"The CDO is the senior executive who bears the overall responsibility for the firm's enterprise-wide data and information strategy, governance, control, policy development and effective exploitation. The CDO's role will combine accountability and responsibility for information protection and privacy, information governance, data quality and data life cycle management, along with the exploitation of data assets to create business value."*

Gartner predicts that most every regulated corporation will have a CDO or equivalent and that 90% + of all Fortune 1000 companies will also have such a dedicated leadership role.

The CDO role is wide, it sits across the whole data value chain:

The Data Value Chain

The skills background of a CDO will likely include:

- steeped in data world
- perhaps with a Business Intelligence /Analytics expertise
- though not necessarily a "techie"
- someone with strategic nous, great stakeholder management skills and commercial flair
- eg 1 recent CDO appointment had 25 yrs experience, had been at data consultancy Dunnhumby for 15yrs, and role there had been as MD / Commercial /Country Mgr, so very immersed in the data world but with strong commercial and c-suite skills
- eg another recent CDO appointment had a PhD in Statistics, had moved from statistician into data analysis /data science and then taking broader responsibilities with more senior data management responsibilities
- a third such example is a CDO with a very strong Computer Science background who was previously the CIO at the same company so knew the company, culture and key people and how to navigate the matrix and politics to get things done!

2. Director of Data Science

AstraZeneca have described their Director of Data Science in this way:

"lead, promote, investigate, develop and implement novel statistical, data mining, machine learning approaches and solutions, skills, capabilities, tools, processes and standard methodologies."

Like many companies they have set up a Data Lab, in their organisation called "The Advanced Analytics Centre" which is their hub of data science experts, integrating historical data compiled from multiple data sources, with local insights from the Marketing teams, to inform new product design and refine trial and execution. The Centre uses advanced predictive techniques and "real-time in-depth multivariate statistical metrics and visualizations for in-flight clinical trial monitoring."

The skills background will need to include:

- excellent understanding of machine learning techniques and algorithms such as kNN, Naïve Bayes, SVM, Decision Forest etc
- experience with common data science tool kits such as R, Weka, Python / NumPy, MatLab etc
- experience with data visualisation tools such as D3.js, GGplot2 etc
- proficiency in using query languages such as SQL, Hive, Pig etc
- understanding of NoSQL databases such as MongoDB, Cassandra and Hbase
- strong statistical skills
- Agile /Scrum/proto-type mind-set /methodology
- potentially also taking in "big data" responsibilities across the whole organisation, eg building a "big data" interrogation environment with eg Hadoop, RapidMiner software skills
- software engineering background
- highly analytical
- someone who enjoys data and detail and the software to understand it.

3. Director of Customer Insight & Analytics

Under Armour describe their Head of Customer Insight & Analytics in this way:

"Determine the shape of UA's future including target markets, product development, marketing investments and marketing messaging.

This individual is the link to the product, brand and category teams who are charged with creating breakthrough product and messaging that engages the needs of our customers. This person is charged to bring the customer profiles, personalities and needs to life within the Company and to the broader organization of category and regional country leads.

Equal part anthropologist, futurist, moderator, influencer and analyst, this senior contributor will be instrumental to driving the intersection of consumer needs to cultural relevance across new wearable technologies, connected fitness, performance wear categories and design style.

A significant part of the work is to guide the sales and marketing teams, to identify most promising leads and customer segments, to evaluate the different parts of the marketing mix and spend and to optimise that spend to maximise the return.

The person is also responsible for linking the consumer to all of the key phases of the innovation lifecycle. The work will span deep qualitative and quantitative immersion, multi-source ideation, trend research and rigorous analytics. The knowledge base / toolkit required of this individual will reflect that diversity of insight needs."

This sort of job description for this role is typically wide-ranging and optimistic! It lands substantial responsibility for growth and innovation onto one core team; provide the analytic-based insight to drive improved customer and consumer engagement and conversion. It does naturally therefore require not just the analytical skills but also outstanding stakeholder manager skills to get the insights that come through adopted, implemented and embraced!

There's a strong business case for investing in this area. According to research from Capgemini:

- 49% of companies who champion the use of analytics are likely to have profit well above their competitors.
- Companies championing the use of customer analytics are 6.5 times more likely to retain customers, 7.4 times more likely to outperform their competitors on making sales to existing customers (upsell and cross sell strategies), and nearly 19 times more likely to achieve above-average profitability.
- The four key areas where integrating customer analytics across the value chain of a business are paying off: enabling integrated multichannel marketing (29%), frontline embedding of analytics (28%), expanding customer analytics across the value chain (27%), and processing real-time data (24%).

Recent appointments in this area will typically see people with many years' experience in analytics, but importantly this will be *customer* analytics and not say pricing risk or fraud analytics which tend to attract people eg with an Actuarial intertest and background. What works best here are those who are also would-be marketers and want to get close to consumers and customers and so would be comfortable reporting into the Chief Marketing Officer or the Chief Data Officer or as in some companies, both!

★★★★★

How do all these roles come together, what sort of Data structure and department should be established which can capture all these core skills and business needs and requirements?

Large scale data teams are still relatively new and have often grown up through a series of independent, not joined-up initiatives with eg both Marketing and IT building their own analytics /data science capability or in the context of a multi-national, each business unit or country market developing their own teams using their local data and each in doing so choosing their own data and analytics platforms, their own governance rules, their own approaches to eg data privacy, instead of there being a joined-up group wide strategy and plan that can capture best practices and synergy and make data work seamlessly across all parts of the organisation.

The org structure here looks at a potential recommended Data function led by the CDO:

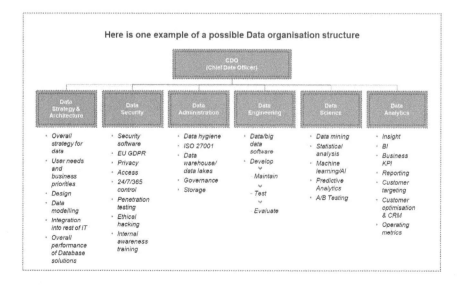

It does embrace all the key skills and components discussed here. It does assume that an organisation will have the budgets and scale to fund the team and resources described. But it is critical to understand that for a Chief Data Officer to do their job, to deliver to expectations, to manage and protect and exploit as the job specs describe, then the CDO does need this sort of team, it does need these skills and these aspects looked after by people with the right experience. And if there were to be compromise then what leave out? Cyber Security? That would be almost negligent. Customer Analytics? That could miss significant new customer revenue opportunities. Each part of the structure is key, and any organisation of size is urged to build as much of this as is affordable and possible.

In terms of reporting lines, research from Gartner and Information Week show that there are many different options and variations:

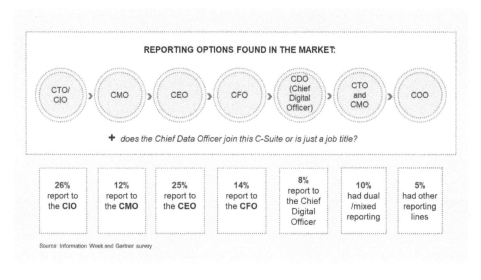

REPORTING OPTIONS FOUND IN THE MARKET:

CTO/CIO → CMO → CEO → CFO → CDO (Chief Digital Officer) → CTO and CMO → COO

✦ does the Chief Data Officer join this C-Suite or is just a job title?

| 26% report to the CIO | 12% report to the CMO | 25% report to the CEO | 14% report to the CFO | 8% report to the Chief Digital Officer | 10% had dual /mixed reporting | 5% had other reporting lines |

Source: Information Week and Gartner survey

★★★★★

The race is on to recruit the best of the talent available in the marketplace. Market feedback shows that good data people are getting recruiter /headhunter calls every week! So for a company to attract the best talent they must be able to demonstrate a genuine commitment to this area, a readiness to invest and have thought through reporting lines and stakeholder interests so they can convince a new recruit that a data leadership role with them can truly make a difference and can succeed. That will be a critical underpinning to turn data into a true driver of RoI and success.

Chapter 4

How Machine Learning is changing the game

For the past 10 /15 years it's been all about Digital. Companies have been urged to go multi-channel, digitise assets, embrace e-commerce, go Mobile, use social media, automate processes, speed up time to market…all an ongoing challenge that's with us to stay.

But even while most companies strive to take advantage of these new ways of working, so a new imperative has recently emerged, one that's just as demanding and yet can additionally provide huge advantage and benefit.

Data Science. Exploiting data to drive rich real-time automated personal insights and competitive advantage. It's not about traditional data management and data warehousing. It's not the time-consuming, high cost, IT-heavy, historic data management taking 2 or 3 years to produce. Now it's about advanced and predictive analytics. It's about using real time data analyses with open source software tools and Cloud-based solutions to deliver the next generation of revenue growth and performance enhancement.

It's the new game-changer and leading-edge companies are starting to invest heavily in this area. Pioneers like Amazon, Uber, NetFlix are now being joined by the likes of Zurich Insurance, Barclays, BT and Mercedes, Pharma and Healthcare, leaders in most every industry, even government agencies, as data science and machine learning go mainstream and become the new source and opportunity for competitive advantage.

Some market stats will help illustrate the significant amount of activity going on in this area:

- The Global Big Data market is expected to grow 5-fold from c. $20bn in 2016 to c. $100bn by 2025

    (Forbes /IDC research)

- It's expected that by 2022, c. 35% of all big data spend will be on advanced Data science /Machine Learning /AI software tools and solutions

    (Reuters)

- "Machine Learning is changing the game. It is enabling enterprises to become more customer-centric, identifying new revenue opportunities, enabling new products and services, creating innovative business models. It's also a major driver of process automation, speed and improving operational performance. These are the dominant factors driving advanced data and analytics investments today. Unleashing the insights hidden in unstructured data is providing enterprises with the potential to compete and improve in areas they had limited visibility into before."

    (Gartner)

- "There's now so much data that we need the machines to process and understand it. At present, it's estimated that less than 1% of all data is ever actually analysed. By 2022, we're expecting a 4300% increase in the amount of data being produced each year."

    (Forbes /IDC)

- Machine Learning /AI start-ups forecast to pick up c.20% of all tech venture capital in 2019

    (Information Week)

Some brief examples to illustrate:

- *Uber* has implemented "dynamic pricing", using machine learning to analyse data in real time and adjust pricing in seconds to reflect existing and anticipated demand
- *McKinsey* has used ML tools to crunch resumes received over the past 30yrs and claim their HR systems can now automatically predict from a resume who will succeed in their firm
- *Quantgene* is using computer-aided diagnosis to spot examples of cancer a year ahead of typical human diagnosis ("today, our biology and medical graduates are also encouraged to be experts in computational and data sciences"),
- *PayPal* uses ML to combat fraud and can now compare millions of transactions in seconds and precisely distinguish between legitimate and fraudulent transactions
- *BT* is using machine learning algorithms and natural language processing to provide real time automated conversations and stand-in for customer service agents
- *STATSports* has launched its new predictive analytics tool: Dynamic Sports Play Prediction", tracking every aspect of player movement in a game, they can simulate every type of possible game situation and predict player reaction and response, so helping ensure "the right player gets picked for the right position in the right game".

With so much development taking place in this area, let's just stand-back and define some key terms.

Some key definitions:

Artificial Intelligence /AI:
- describes any technique that enables computers to mimic human intelligence using logic, if-then rules, decision trees and machine learning

Machine Learning:
- at its simplest, this is about using machines to crunch vast amounts of data, increasingly in real-time, to gather new insights
- at its more complex, it's about using statistical techniques that enable machines to improve at tasks with experience

Deep Learning
- is a "subset" of ML and is about developing algorithms that enable the software to train itself to perform tasks like speech and image recognition.

All this AI /ML/DL technology is able to develop insights and do things that are beyond human capabilities. It is based on the patterns it can derive from crunching vast amounts of big data, very quickly. It can for example anticipate a shopper's future needs based on their history and adjust their user /buying experience in real time to reflect that, it can predict candidate suitability for jobs, enable "internet of things" type opportunities with eg Mercedes exploring how automotive systems might automatically monitor performance, report errors and fix problems, it can automatically organise collections of photos on your mobile phone, it's enabling chat bots in call centres, it can be seen as a cost reduction tool (eg Google have used it to cut 15% of the costs of running their data centres), but it can also be seen as a generator of new sources of business opportunity.

Amazon's Alexa is one example. Here's how the team at Amazon describe what they are doing:

"The Alexa Data Science and Machine Learning team made the magic of Alexa possible, but that was just the beginning. Our goal is to make voice interfaces ubiquitous and as natural as speaking to a human. We have a relentless focus on the customer experience and customer feedback. We use many real-world data sources including customer interactions and a variety of techniques like highly scalable deep learning. Learning at this massive scale requires new research and development. The team is responsible for cutting-edge research and development in virtually all fields of Human Language Technology: Automatic Speech Recognition (ASR), Artificial Intelligence (AI), Natural Language Understanding (NLU), Question Answering, Dialog Management, and Text-to-Speech (TTS)."

-(Amazon VP Rohit Prasad)

Let's look at applications of these technologies in 3 areas:

- Contact /Call centres
- Marketing
- Insurance Services

1. How AI/ML is transforming call centres

Today's contact and call centres are already using Digital tools to communicate. Not just phone but via social media, instant messaging, video conference and web chat. It need be no great step then for call centres to eventually replace human interaction with bots powered by AI.

Gartner predicts that by 2022, 85% of all customer interactions will no longer be managed by people but by bots. The likes of Facebook, Apple, Microsoft have all built and deployed virtual assistants and chatbots which can respond to voice queries and engage in an increasingly natural dialogue and especially able to deal with a growing list of most frequently asked questions.

In theory, it's argued, virtual assistants will "improve the customer experience because the AI bots can store endless amounts of data and access the most relevant information at the right time to give customer exactly what they want.". Adopting this approach is also seen as a major boost to efficiency and reducing costs of 24/7 global call centre operations.

There are questions about the acceptability of this approach to people calling-up for help, whether bots can replace tele-sales, the "naturalness of the language", the absence of any humour or genuine human contact and concern, and whether bots will be more time efficient or might in fact take longer to resolve a problem. But a recent research report from Oracle shows that 41% of Customer Experience Officers and heads of call centre departments expect their use of bots to significantly increase, especially as AI/ML technology continues to evolve and improve. In fact in a recent report from Xerox, 42% of execs said they expected the contact centre as we know it now will cease to exist by 2025.

2. How AI/ML is transforming Marketing

Moo.com is a provider of on-demand printing services and is currently exploring the world of machine learning and AI, especially when it comes to Marketing.

They started with replacing the static FAQs on their website. They put in place an automated ML solution which can review past and current customer behaviour on their sites to learn and update what content and information was popular and most relevant. This has enabled Moo.com to keep fine-tuning their site to reflect what customers are most interested in.

They have been able to build on that capability to now provide an Amazon. com type personalisation engine to tailor individual customer experience online that best fits each customer's needs.

Moo.com believe that this initiative has by itself helped drive continuing increases in revenue (they now operate across Europe and the US) as well as providing more effective self-serve customer solutions.

TGI Fridays is another example. They have introduced "chatbots" based on ML/AI to personalise their interaction with their customers. It means that at any time any customer can have an apparently 1-1 conversation with TGI about menus, pricing, nearest restaurant, location details, special offers, allergy advice and so on. With every chatbot interaction, each customer also receives happy hour suggestions and special offers. They also now have added a home delivery capability.

Sherif Mityas was the CIO at TGI at the time launching this initiative: "We wanted to be part of the conversation when people are discussing where to go out and get recommendations. We saw a 500% increase in engagement with customers on social media channels since deploying this new conversation-based customer experience. It's a huge win for the brand".

TGI and Moo worked with the data science firm StatWolf. Based in Ireland, they developed the bespoke software tools and worked with the companies on the implementation and monitoring of the marketing and customer impact the technology was having. There are now many others consultancies and agencies providing similar services from the majors like IBM, Accenture and Cognizant to start-up and more entrepreneurial ventures and agencies like Data Reply, Applied AI and Evolution AI. They can all provide low cost proto-type solutions that enable companies to explore the potential without having to incur substantial expenditure up-front.

A report by Gleanster, the US Marketing research firm, found that 90% of companies expected to use more marketing automation in the next 5 yrs. This can include everything from email marketing, social media monitoring, search engine optimisation to align with changes in search algorithms at Google, content distribution, programmatic advertising as well the type of ML initiatives seen at Moo and TGI.

In particular companies are looking at how ML can deliver customer loyalty and secure long- term customer retention, And key to this is developing personalised marketing based not on past data and previous campaigns but using data analysis and insight to better understand and determine future customer needs, what does the customer want, what will excite and drive higher levels of engagement and spend. This can mean dynamic ad-copy, customised call centre and online experience, personalised recommendations, anticipated "time of need", dynamic pricing, one-to-one conversations carried across desktop and mobile…AI making "hyper-personalisation at scale".

3. How AI/ML is changing Insurance

In a recent KPMG report, they comment that: "the opportunities to apply ML tools and solutions in the insurance industry are especially significant". Insurance organisations are founded on Data and most have already digitised existing records. It is also a resource intensive business where processes like claims administration are time-consuming and often a frustrating experience for customers.

KPMG suggest Insurers could use Machine Learning to drive two key areas of improvement across the data value chain: (i) reduction in costs and (ii) enhanced competitiveness.

The Data Science Value Chain

Source: Digital-360

By automating and using ML, it's reckoned that insurers could cut claims processing times down from a number of months to a matter of minutes. It's also estimated that because ML should be more accurate than human judgement on claims, so it could cut out the number of denied claims which often result in appeals and then a subsequent settlement. All that aspect of the claims process could be eliminated.

In terms of improved competitiveness, KPMG customer research suggests that people might pay a premium for a product that guarantees "frictionless claims payout" without the hassle of having to have long and protracted call centre and email claims discussions. It's argued that this whole drive towards simplicity, faster response, easier interaction could also significantly increase customer retention and loyalty, reinforced by simple quick renewal.

For KPMG, the benefits of applying ML across the Insurance sector are overwhelming and yet they see very slow uptake.

The reasons appear to be a mix of "other priorities right now", "we're concerned it won't make the difference that's claimed", and perhaps more pointedly: "we haven't thought through the people issues around wholesale automation and whether we're ready to implement such radical and sweeping changes".

This last point is something that many established businesses, and not just in Insurance, are grappling with. No-one is now doubting the power and potential of AI. We can all see how for new pure play companies like an Uber or a NetFlix, with no established people-based ways of working, so it's easier for them to move quickly to a technology-led solution. But where a company employs perhaps thousands of people eg in a claims department, the migration from "people-led" to "tech-led" becomes harder in both cultural /emotional terms as well as in the transformation required to migrate often decades-old established processes and ways of working.

KPMG accept this point in their survey and talk about "overcoming cultural differences" as the key challenge especially for long-established Insurance organisations. Without doubt, insurers have typically not been early adopters of new technologies but what should now make the transformation journey easier is the ability to experiment with ML solutions in a low cost experimental way. Trialling initiatives that can be regarded as a necessary piece of "siloed innovation", a way of finding out and exploring what possible in a small part of the business, perhaps a recent development area itself which might lend itself more readily to some radical change.

Picking an area which is data intensive, where there is a lot of routine and repetitive tasks, where there are perhaps already proven ML solutions in the market that a specialist data agency can adapt for this organisation, all that can make the first steps easier to manage and negotiate. Once there's proof of concept of course the business case becomes more persuasive and the easier perhaps to make changes that can capture the RoI.

★★★★★

Recent McKinsey analysis looking at the potential of Machine Learning has concluded and not unexpectedly that there are opportunities across most every industry sector. And these opportunities are all around using data and analytics in the ways described and illustrated above: real time data insights, personalisation, automation, predictive analytics to identify new revenue opportunities, the reduction /elimination of repetitive tasks...from simple cost-cutting to developing new business models, ML is providing a whole new playing field for companies to find new sources of competitive advantage.

Machine learning has great impact potential across industries and use case types

Impact potential Low ▭ High

Problem type	Automotive	Manufacturing	Consumer	Finance	Agriculture	Energy	Health care	Pharma-ceuticals	Public/social	Media	Telecom	Transport and logistics
Real-time optimization												
Strategic optimization												
Predictive analytics												
Predictive maintenance												
Radical personalization												
Discover new trends/anomalies												
Forecasting												
Process unstructured data												

SOURCE: McKinsey Global Institute analysis

While there's a lot of concern with all of this technology about the future workplace and robots replacing people, we can end this chapter with a positive conclusion from a recent PWC report:

"Since we're all going to be living longer, it's a good thing that bots will help many of us live richer and more fulfilling lives. By reducing labour costs – robots work tirelessly and don't demand raises – automation will make existing companies more profitable and perhaps most importantly spur the creation of new ones. It's estimated that AI could boost domestic GDP by 10% over the coming decade. In the UK that could add c. £230bn to GDP by 2030 and in the US add c.$2 trillion or more. And with that, create many new jobs. Automation can make existing jobs more fulfilling and with effective training and retraining the data economy can herald an exciting new era for all of us".

Chapter 5

InsurTech case study: how AI/ML is changing the game

FinTech /InsurTech is at the forefront of how Machine Learning and Artificial Intelligence is changing the game. New data tools are providing the ability to analyse vast amounts of information, in real time, and so automate decision-making. As just discussed in the last chapter, it can drive superior cost efficiency as eg claims processing gets automated and most especially the ability to precisely target customers and consumers with the policies they need, when they need them, tailored for them and at a price that is compelling.

A good case study is Simply Business. Here's an insurance company that started up in 2010 and by 2019 had become the UK market leader in providing B2B insurance for small /medium enterprises. They have been working to integrate machine learning and attendant techniques into their everyday business. Though at the same time, they still strongly also believe in human decision-making and see automation as an adjunct to that, rather than as a replacement…"we're not interested in replacing people with algorithms, particularly when we're dealing with clients as personal and unique as the UK's small businesses. Instead, we want to find ways to put technology in the service of our customers and of our own employees."

Simply Business ("SB") have a large contact centre based in Northampton and they use that channel vigorously encouraging customers to call and be in touch. But the volume of calls can be considerable and so they developed a new model to give the tools to prioritise telephone leads based on all the information they had about a customer – the type of business, their revenue, the age of the business, and so on. Crucially, it also prioritises based on their existing interactions, such as their time on the web site, the number of pages they visited, the channels they came through to SB, and more.

SB can now track and prioritise prospects in far more efficient ways. For example, as soon as a visitor arrives on their web site, machine learning will give them a priority score. This score changes based on engagement with the site – it's constantly updated, depending on how the user behaves. They're then placed into one of eight groups, from 'most likely' to convert to 'least likely'.

This new data/insight tool has had a concrete impact on marketing strategy. SB has learnt how to identify leads with the lowest likelihood of conversion, and can instead invest time and marketing money in providing even more tailored messaging to those more likely to convert – and it's led to double digit improvements.

SB are also using machine learning on the content side. Their Knowledge Centre is an important acquisition and engagement driver, but it now also uses ML to serve the most useful recommended articles to specific segments in a seamless way, recommending the right article to each customer – and that's also led to improved customer conversion and results.

SB are not alone in pioneering these new techniques, but the insurance sector generally has been traditional and resistant to change, and this is why AI can have a greater impact there than perhaps in other more customer-centric data-sophisticated sectors like Retail and Telco. The new ways to collect and interrogate data of new types and the use of new algorithms are disrupting the sector in several ways.

Traditionally, an insurance company followed this type of process:

- Identifying pool of customers who might be risk-assessed;
- Targeting those customers and assessing the risk for each class;
- Selling differently priced policies spreading the risks over the pool of customers;
- Try to retain those customers as long as possible offering lower price for longer contracts.

This is a really simplistic representation of the insurance business in the last fifty years but the insurance industry can be characterized as "product-led" rather than "customer-led"; products and services have been *sold not bought*, price has been the key determinant, rather than true customer service and the customer /market data has often been owned by brokers and agents and now often the comparison price aggregators all of whom have been essential to tracking new customers and to even retain old ones. In addition, it is an industry which is by definition rich in data because they have collected anything they could, but is also one of the less advanced because much of that data is unstructured or semi-structured, or the IT system model used quite old and simple.

While Insurers have implemented many initiatives to better engage with customers, the process used in the insurance business has not changed as much. *Expert systems* and *knowledge engineering* have dominated the sector setting the rules to be followed in internal workflows, but this is slowly changing with intelligent automation systems. And can now see examples of actually migrating from rule-based decision systems to statistical learning and eventually machine learning.

AI is helping (or disrupting!) the sector in different ways. First of all, it can help increase the customer engagement and retention. The abundance of data can be used indeed to refine the customers' segmentation and provide personalized offers based on personal features. It also helps in reducing the costs through process automation.

Second, AI is making people more aware of the risks as well as habits, and it is driving them toward better behaviours. Furthermore, the better pricing and risk assessment that AI is introducing analysing more granular data will give greater clarity on risks and people that are uninsurable (i.e. too risky to be fairly priced and covered) as well as to turn back some previously uninsurable people into insurable customers again.

With a better and more detailed customer profiling and a more insight into risk management, it will improve ability to forecast and compute both the probability and magnitude of potential claims and losses even in those cases too hard to be managed before. All the data insight improvements should result in lower average premiums, lower the threshold of what we consider nowadays an insurable risk and make more risks insurable.

This intersection of AI and Insurance is seeing a tremendous level of new business/start-up venture/innovation activity and helpful to look at least at some of them to understand the future direction of the industry, as well as the kind of game-changing potential improvements AI is having in the InsurTech space. An interesting thing to notice is that a lot of the core innovation is happening in the UK rather than other countries, in all the segments described below.

Claim processing: *Shift Technology* skims the valid claims from the ones that deserve further validations; *Tractable* is trying to automate specified key tasks for insurers; *ControlExpert* has a specific focus on car claims; *Cognotekt* optimises internal business processes, as well as *Snapsheet* does; *Motionscloud* offers instead mobile claim management solutions; and *RightIndem* aims to help insurers to deliver on-premise, smoothing the claiming flow.

Virtual Agents & Chatbots: *Spixii* is an automated insurance agent who helps you buying any insurance coverage you might want; *Cognicor* is a virtual assistant that offers customer care services; *Conversica* identifies which leads intend to purchase, while *Your.MD* is a personal health assistant that analyses symptoms and produces pieces of advice. *MedWhat* instead uses EMR (medical records) to assist the patient as a virtual doctor, and *Babylon* gives medical advice taking care of tight budget constraints. *Insurify* is another personal insurance agent who works as a comparator, in their case for car insurances.

What today is called simply chatbot is gradually being redesignated as *robo-insurer*. There are already examples of companies moving toward that goal: *Risk Genius* is an "intelligent comparator" which identifies gaps in coverage for the customer and *PolicyGenius* looks for the best solution that fits customer's needs and characteristics, while *DriveSpotter* implements real-time video analytics to keep drivers safe(r). More generally, robo-insurers will be a quite wide class of agents who will end up providing different services, all of them with the final goal of helping the clients to undertake risk-mitigating actions and only cover the real (residual) risks.

Customers engagement: *Oscar* is one of the more successful InsurTech companies out there, with the final goal of making insurance simple and accessible to everyone through a great UX. Similar to Oscar is *Stride Health*, while *Brolly* is a tool that helps customers in understanding their own needs and facilitates in one place all the insurance coverages, in a similar fashion to *Knip*. *Adtelligence* instead creates personalised offers and relevant products based on a customer's characteristics. *Captricity* uses machine learning to convert handwritten files into structured data, and this can be used to better understand the final customer. Finally, *ValChoice* ranks the service of insurers to the benefit of the client.

Telematics*: connected cars and telematics is a significant area in its own right, but it would be worth highlighting the work that *Greenroad, Vnomics*, and *Fleetmatics* (now part of Verizon) are doing in also capturing driving behaviours and habits as well as computing fuel efficiency. *Cambridge Mobile Telematics* works similarly, although it uses smartphone data and mobile devices habits. *Navdy* is trying to revolutionise the UI/UX within vehicles, displaying information in such a way that the driver does not get distracted. *Lytx* uses vision technology to provide real-time feedbacks to the driver.

Underwriting*: AI can be used to spot out hidden correlations to segment customers and risks in a more efficient way. Many companies operate in the space, as for instance *Carpe Data* that provides predictive algorithms and data products for property and casualty/general and life insurances through the analysis of public data (e.g., social media data). *Atidot* created a machine learning risk management platform, while *Tyche Risk* uses unstructured data to optimize the underwriting and claims process. *Big Cloud Analytics* collects data from wearables and formulates health scores for a better risk assessment, while *Cape Analytics* uses computer vision techniques on geospatial data to improve the level of detail on current houses conditions. *Dreamquark* creates a more accurate representation of the medical datasets to be used for underwriting purposes by insurances, similarly to *FitSense* that offers also apps products. *Melody Health Insurance* provides also low-cost insurances, while *Uvamo* uses AI to assess the risk of policy applications. A more accurate underwriting can even translate into covering events that are today quite risky (e.g. as *Meteo Protect* and *Praedicat* are doing for weather risk management).

It is also useful to point to pure technological enablers such as *Instanda*, which offers a management tool to insurance providers to manage effectively new products launched; *Insly,* a cloud-based platform for insurance brokers; and *SimpleInsurance* is an e-commerce provider for product insurances.

P2P insurance*: Lemonade, Friendsurance,* and *Guevara* are peer-to-peer insurance start-ups focusing respectively on property and casualty/general insurance and car insurance.

Insurchain & Smart Contracts*: these are companies in the insurance sector that are driven by *blockchain technology*. *Elliptic* monitors for fraud on crypto-currencies, while *Everledger* is a permanent immutable ledger for diamond certification. *Luther Systems* is an enterprise blockchain technology venture working on the standardisation of smart contracts. *Dynamis* provides a P2P supplementary unemployment insurance product, while *Saldo* provides micro-insurance policies on blockchain. *SafeShare* covers multiple parties with insurance cover at short notice and for varying periods, and finally, *Teambrella* is another P2P insurance platform run on blockchain.

Insurance on-demand: this class of start-ups puts in customers' hand the entire insurance buying process. *Trov* is probably the best example of this new class of players and it allows to ensure things by simply taking a picture of them. *Cuvva* is quite similar but with a focus on car insurance, *Sure* and *Airsurety* on travel policies, and *Back me up* is another example of on-demand insurance. But this group includes not only the on-demand business model, but also start-ups which provide products that vary by location, time, use, or customer. In other words, pay-per-mile business model (*Metromile*), micro-insurance policies (*Neosurance*), or eventually Insurance-as-a-service models (*Digital Risks*).

In sum, there are four elements which constitute the insurance profit structure: premium earned and the investment income on one hand, and underwriting cost and claim expenses on the other. AI is and will be able to improve the cost structure, increasing at the same time the competitiveness and enlarging the customer base accessible to insurers, while optimising internal processes and enhancing the transparency and robustness of the compliance flow. The greatest challenge is the cultural mindset inside the large global established insurance groups. That may delay adoption of early AI solutions, though the significant pressure to innovate may well accelerate more of this InsurTech innovation.

Chapter 6

The still untapped potential of effective Customer Data & Analytics

A few recent headlines:

"GSK (Glaxo) announce partnership with McLaren Formula 1 motor racing to access their expertise in big data analytics"

"ASOS.com and Shop Direct unlock the value of real-time analytics"

"IBM now have a team of c. 15,000 worldwide focussed on Data & Analytics"

"American Express forges new customer relationships through deep analysis and research"

"Uber, Amazon, Netflix have been pioneers in data science, machine learning and predictive analytics, they are now being joined by a host of others"

"Alexander Stojanovic, VP at eBay, describes how analytics is at the heart of their key business decision-making"

"Beth Butterwick, CEO at Karen Millen, has commented: "if we truly understand the customer data, understand the journey from beginning to end, then we have the strategic horsepower to influence the entire organisation"

★★★★★

Few doubt the value of analysis to drive better decision-making. In these days where there is a "deluge of available data" there is a growing imperative to find ways to capture, interrogate and find the key insights that can drive competitive advantage.

However, a recent study from the Aberdeen Group showed that a surprising 78%! of company executives felt that their organisations "struggled to make effective use of customer data". At the same time, those who were able to master customer analysis and insight showed remarkable results. They could point to increases in:

- net new customer revenues
- revenues from customer referrals
- cross-sell and upsell gains
- plus improvements in annual % customer service costs.

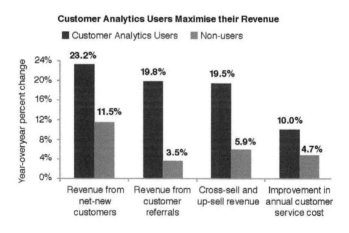

Customer Analytics Users Maximise their Revenue

The winners, the "customer data masters", are companies like Starbucks, Amazon, Wells Fargo, Sainsbury's, Citibank, Adidas. And success is not only the preserve of large multi-nationals; smaller local companies can also take advantage without spending $Ms to do so. Here's a few case study examples:

Adidas: Lia Vakoutis, Senior Director at Adidas, has described how they have mined social media data to drive new product sales:

"We used to prepare promotions months in advance. Because of the cost and time invested we used to just roll them out hoping they'd work ok. But if they didn't it was too late to do much to change. So we made a decision to move from "reactive marketing" to "predictive marketing".

"To achieve this shift in Marketing and promotions planning, we now use a variety of tools to monitor social media sentiment including SalesForce Radian 6 (social media /Marcomms monitoring in real time), Sysomos (provider of infographics and reports on competitive social media performance), Crimson Hexagon (manages /analyses big data). All these can work together to produce the most detailed picture of what's going on in our social media world"

Adidas focus on 4 key social media fora: Twitter, YouTube, Facebook and Instagram.

They are analysing for example some 1200 soccer specific message boards, blogs, new sites. A recent campaign count showed they had analysed over 4 million pieces of information across 17 markets in multiple languages. Because the analysis and insights are coming through in real time, Adidas can shift promotions, feature the sports stars who are getting more traction and response, change promotional material, add or change copy, influence conversations and also react immediately to competitor activity. "It's just a brilliant way to test what works and what does not, and be able to react instantaneously. In one recent campaign we were able to test and monitor 300 different concepts in one 48 hour period".

Amazon.com: Amazon are so often cited these days as best practice, but when I interviewed them, they spoke about the following:

"Of all the things we do today, we believe it's our *real time customer analytics that make the difference.*

We have a team monitoring customer activity by the second and we can see immediately what's working, what's not, we can identify price change opportunities, page lay-out changes, product-bundling and we can check this across all users and our whole customer base".

"What really makes this data monitoring work is that we *use* it and make the changes in real time too. How do we do that? We have a "virtual circle" of Analytics, UX/Conversion and Web Dev. That is made up of three core groups of people who work very actively together. They are co-located, they report to one person, they are the key commercial grouping".

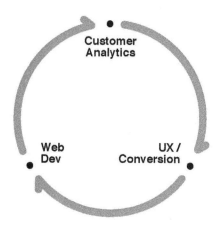

That sort of real-time analytical *plus* change capability is rare. Some companies with similar fast-moving /fashion /consumer-driven businesses do try to organise in this way. For example retailers John Lewis and Next. But what even these successful organisations lack is that corresponding real-time change capability. They still impose too many checks and controls to make that work easily.

One more case study comparing *Starbucks* with *Pret a Manger*.

Starbucks introduced its customer loyalty scheme some 10 yrs ago. It is recognised as being the most successful loyalty program in the USA. The My Starbucks rewards program started as a simple payment card before it gradually evolved into the successful rewards scheme it is today ("one sip gets you gold status").

Howard Schultz, when CEO and then Chairman, updated shareholders at an AGM: "More than half of My Starbucks's 15.3 million members are high-spending gold members, in addition more than 23 million use the mobile-payments app and in one quarter alone more than $2bn was loaded by members onto their cards"

"We can do all this and make it easy for members because we have invested in building our customer database and capability. It means that we can see what our members are doing and critically these days we can personalise and tailor all our customer communications so each member can feel some personal connection with us".

Starbucks uses Oracle Siebel customer relationship management (CRM) software as its loyalty system, which is tied to the Oracle ERP platform. This delivers a combination of transactional, analytical and engagement features to manage all the sources of customer data, no matter if it's in-store or on mobile. That ties into their cloud-based Oracle "Exadata" data warehouse for scale.

Starbucks has massive amounts of data that needs continuous cleansing and analysis and with c. 4 billion+ cups of coffee sold each year that is a lot of data! "...and we still have not been able to get all the insights out that are possible".

Pret a Manger on the other hand has taken a very different approach to customer loyalty. Instead of building extensive customer databases, their approach is to leave loyalty up to each employee's discretion. "We looked at loyalty cards but did not want to spend all that money building up some large scale Clubcard-style analysis". Instead, the Pret approach is described as "freestyle and fun" empowering employees to give away eg free coffees.

On the one hand, Pret has received praise for its innovative approach and it certainly ties into the company's culture. But critics point out that such freebies are arbitrary and whimsical and easy for genuine loyal customers to be ignored and overlooked. Also it's pointed-out that the lack of customer data insight might surely disadvantage Pret in the long term as more data-driven schemes work to develop that ever closer customer connection and relationship?

★★★★★

With these sort of case studies showing what possible and what can be achieved, why is that 78% of executives in the Aberdeen Group research are frustrated with their own company's lack of progress in this area?

A recent Harvard Business Review study showed that 53% of execs surveyed by them felt that: "getting the customer experience right" was an important strategic priority (one wonders about the other 47% who did not agree with that statement!). But there was a broad consensus about the key challenges to be overcome:

(i) *Proving the RoI*: companies find that while there can be many customer improvement initiatives it can be difficult to clearly attribute and show which initiative is delivering what RoI and this makes further investment cases hard to validate. So half of the companies in the HBR survey said that: "it's still a struggle to fund customer experience programs"

(ii) *"Deluge of data"*: "there's now so much potential data available but what are we going to do with it all?"

(iii)*Multi-channel complexity*: "we are looking at data from web, store, email, social media, tele-sales, call centre, field sales, Mobile, customer query handling, past purchase records…even assuming we capture all this data accurately, which we don't, then how do we get to a unified view?"

(iv)*Data integration /standardisation*: Only 18% of companies in the HBR survey felt that they had an integrated data capture system. "We have different departments operating in silos with their own databases and drawing their own conclusions. Efforts to tie the data together meet 100 reasons why not".

(v) *Lack of key skills*: Is there a Chief Data Officer? If there is, how much of that person's time is deep in data science, or do they also work to drive the insights into the Marketing and customer decision-making process? Is each of the areas in the Customer value chain effectively being staffed and led? Is that whole chain of value being brought together, coordinated and championed by one senior Data/Analytics /Insight Officer?

(vi)*No unifying Dashboard /metrics /KPi:* Both in the HBR and the previously mentioned Aberdeen Group surveys, a key reason cited for lack of progress was the absence of a clear set of metrics and KPi. There was no agreed measures of what was successful customer experience, there was no comparison of how well the company was doing vs. competitors in this area or vs. more widely relevant benchmarks, no way of identifying and agreeing what was working and what not, no insight to show what the improvement gaps might be, no understanding of what the full potential could be if customer engagement was truly optimised.

(vii) *No use of NPS:* NPS or Net Promoter Score is fast becoming the global standard for measuring how well a company is delivering on customer service. It's descrbed in more detail here in chapter 10. It's a system pioneered by Bain Consulting and Satmetrix. Its power lies in the monitoring and measuring the NPS trend and benchmarking vs competition.

Those who embrace NPS see it as the key catalyst and start of their Customer Analytics journey. "It's an objective market study, it shows how we're doing and it compares our performance, it has galvanised us into defining what other metrics we needed and how to go about getting that data and insight together".

★★★★★

Let's look at two company cases studies where they seem to have effectively managed their way through these significant challenges:

Countax are a great independent manufacturing benchmark, countax. co.uk. They produce lawnmowers, UK-based, distributing worldwide, just 120 staff. Darren Spencer, one of the senior Directors, commented: "Our business had long suffered with insufficient or difficult to access data across all aspects of our operation and especially in better understanding our distributor and end-user customer base. Quick access to information we trusted was just not possible. We had the data, we just couldn't use it or it was very painful to get it!"

Countax hired a Business Intelligence software firm called Matillion who set about implementing a SaaS data warehouse solution which would integrate with their ERP as well as with other in-house developed bespoke systems. The areas of BI and data integration covered Sales, Inventory, Supply Chain, Customer Data and customer purchase /contact history. Data inputs and definitions were defined, the key dashboard metrics were agreed and a major effort took place to unify and standardise so there would be a single and common view of all the data insights.

Now Countax has a self-service BI environment which is designed at various levels of detail so that even the non-data literate can access, interpret and digest. "The reporting ability that comes from this business intelligence has greatly helped. We now rely on these analyses to guide the strategic direction; we didn't have this level of visibility before. And because we have a common dashboard it makes our management meetings much quicker and easier, there's no debate about the data, it's now simply about what actions to take…wish we had done this years ago!"

Sainsbury's: CEO Mike Coupe sees customer data analytics as the key to the company's future success: "We are aiming for a future where we know every single customer on an intimate basis…we want to be able to predict what our customers will need, when they'll need and how best to deliver that to them".

Sainsbury's has been on a long journey collecting and building "a vault of customer data". But in its early days that information was accessible to only a few analysts and coders. " We weren't using the information to its full capacity, it wasn't easily accessible to Buying, Merchandising and Marketing and so we were short of the customer insights needed to break new ground",

Sainsbury's teamed up with Aimia (and subsequently acquired them!). Aimia are customer analytics /loyalty specialists, and together developed a 6-point strategy and change programme:

(i) *Identify the key metrics*: This was a critical step: what are the key measures of effective customer engagement and how be sure to measure those things that can truly drive sales. Sainsbury's has developed a wide list of these KPi which include basics such as trends in average spend, basket size, frequency of purchase, customer lifetime value etc to derive a "loyalty index" and allies with that with more emotional /sentiment scores derived from research, online surveys, social media and NPS scores. All this done not just at a store level but where possible at an individual customer level.

(ii) *Train staff, continuously, in Customer Service*

(iii) *Build a dedicated team*: now c. 120+ people responsible for customer data management, analysis, reporting and insight. Reports are tailored for each department so eg Buying will get its own set of analyses and insights as well as seeing the bigger picture.

(iv) *Monitor use of the data insights.* A key task of all senior managers is to ensure the data insights are followed through and actioned.

(v) *Personalisation*: Develop customer marketing and promotion campaigns and initiatives that allow individualised, personalised customer comms.

(vi) *Supplier investment*: Sainsbury's has worked with its supplier base to give them access to this customer data and insights. The aim is to help suppliers identify what sells best, innovate and develop products that customers want, see which promotions work best and generally enable them to maximise their own business activities.

In a recent statement, CEO Mike Coupe has re-emphasised the need to continue to invest in this area: "It's on-going to address the changing and multi-channel needs of customers. So we want to still improve the in-store customer experience with further investment in staff training and a new automated system to track availability. We are also committing to further systems infrastructure to create a single view of customers, leading to increasingly effective interactions"

★★★★★

Whether it's Sainsbury's, Starbucks, Netflix, Countax or John Lewis, whether B2C or B2B, in today's highly competitive world, companies are of course having to work harder to grow and be successful. Few would argue that "developing an intimate understanding of our customer" is not a major imperative and need.

The challenge is to establish that company-wide commitment to getting those data analyses and insights together in a unified form that can drive decision-making and enhanced customer engagement. Will future Aberdeen Group surveys continue to show 78% of companies struggling to build an effective customer analytics platform?

Chapter 7

Digital and Data Transformation: 10 keys to success

Research group Forrester has been tracking the amount of *digital and data transformation* activity and investment taking place. They are finding it's now the No. 1 CEO agenda item.

They cite the following as a typical example:

Craig Menear, CEO of The Home Depot, recently shared a plan to spend $100 million on digital technology so customers could order on their phones and pick up in the store. Six months later, he raised that to $1billion to cover additional investment in new automated distribution centers, an overhauled fulfillment process, real-time inventory management to facilitate immediate customer services and better online ordering.

Home Depot is becoming a case study example of how a company can transform itself from a traditional bricks n' mortar retailer to a successful omni-channel organisation. Its share price is up 300% over the past 5 yrs.

As Craig Menear sums up: "we must continue to invest to transform this business…we recognise the front door of our store is no longer in-store, it's in the customer's home, in their pocket, on the job site…if we don't transform ourselves then someone's going to eat our lunch".

The Forrester conclusion is that: "Businesses must double-down now on their investment in technology-led transformation. Companies are finding they need to spend $4 on operational excellence for every $1 investment in digital customer experience. Now it's all about transforming the *total* corporation every day to make it fit for purpose for the next decade."

And as Adobe CEO Shantanu Narayen has crisply put it: *"if we don't reinvent then someone will reinvent us out of business"*

With this great pressure to transform, what are the lessons learned among the more successful corporations, how have they driven that change, how have they galvanised the workforce to embrace new ways of working, new processes and new priorities, how get the return on that transformation investment?

This research described here has looked at many companies across a number of industries, in retail, financial services, telco and others. Companies have been examined for how and why they have failed, as much as looking at winners who have succeeded. Key organisation transformation journeys at the likes of Adobe, Barclays, Aviva, RELX, Syngenta, Sprint, Citi Group, ING Bank, UPS, Novartis, AstraZeneca and a number of others have all been examined. The research is now highlighting the following 10 keys that can drive success. They are:

The 10 keys driving successful digital business transformation:

1. *An overriding vision and strategy*
2. *CEO personal full-time involvement*
3. *Streamlined objectives*
4. *Inject the voice of the customer*
5. *Emphasise /dramatise the urgency*
6. *Agile ways of working*
7. *Break down silos*
8. *Town hall comms*
9. *Investor management*
10. *Link everyone's pay and benefits*

Let's consider each briefly in turn:

1. An overriding vision and strategy

Here's one startling example, from a recent speech by Chinese Premier Xi Jinping: *"We will become the global leader in data and AI…supremacy in artificial intelligence (AI) is very important"*. China has announced plans to draw level with the US by 2020 and to dominate global AI by 2030.

As Ed Luce of the FT has commented: "China is already ahead of its Silicon Valley counterparts in areas like online payments, e-Commerce, visual recognition, voice software, it is fast catching-up on driverless cars. Today the US is the world's technology leader. With China's new stated vision and investment tomorrow may look very different".

It's this type of vision-setting which can be so powerful, to set that target and set of goals for the total organisation. In the business landscape, there are a number of powerful case studies of this kind of far-reaching strategy.

For example, at Home Depot: to be the No. 1 omni-channel retailer in the US, or at Adobe: to transform from a traditional desktop software company to an always-on online services subscription business, or at Elsevier: to move from publishing education books to an information services software provider, or at TUI, the world's largest holiday tour operator: to transform from an intermediary selling hotel and flights on behalf of others to now becoming the tour destination owner in its own right, or at UPS: to have the most advanced parcel tracking real time data capability of any company in the world, whether that be FedEx or Amazon and where they have committed an ongoing annual capital investment of $1bn to sustain that, or at SAP: to become the world's largest cloud-based software solutions vendor…all these companies have found that the setting of a vision that is *"challenging, inspiring and stretching but just about achievable"* has been a critical catalyst to action.

2. CEO personal full-time leadership

The Adobe CEO Shantanu Narayen is a good exemplar of this. Having set their strategy and goals, Narayen put the transformation programme out there as the No. 1 company priority.

He did a tremendous amount of communication around that but the thing that people at Adobe most remember and comment on is the following. Wherever he went, no matter which facility or country or business unit, he would ask the same question to people he passed in the corridor, or who found themselves in the elevator with him or at the water-cooler: what are you working on today, is it directly involved in the transformation, if it isn't then stop it, now, and redirect your time and energies.

Underpinning this priority was a core set of KPi and metrics very linked to the transformation goals and each person in the organisation had their own personal KPi related to that.

Another example comes from Steve Hughes, CEO of the Principality Building Society (the largest in Wales, sixth largest in the UK). "As CEO, I'm focussed on defining the mission and culture of our organisation and for me walking the talk is key". Steve is an example of an extraordinary commitment to engage the whole company in the strategy and ambition and to inspire each employee, going round all 71 branches, speaking to hundreds of members / customers, sharing plans and ideas and then *consistently* doing that to get everyone aligned around their future plans.

3. Streamlined objectives

When Adam Crozier as CEO took charge of ITV (the UK news, content and entertainments business), he found the company facing a digital storm with collapsing traditional broadcasting advertising revenues, a loss of confidence among the staff and critically too a loss of faith among the investment community. It was described as "one of the most challenging of corporate turnarounds".

Four years later, the company's market cap had quintupled to nearly £9bn and it became one of the stars of the FTSE 100. Job done, Adam has since moved on (now Chair at Asos.com and at Whitbread), but a strong platform for the future has been built and even with continuing intense global competition and economic uncertainties, the core businesses of Studios and Online continue to report good annual growth.

What happened? ITV articulated the bold vision of a news service completely rebuilt around the principle of 'digital first'. Leapfrogging several generations of developments in online news, ITV set out a radical plan to build the structure of its news website around a feed of live updates which could in turn be aggregated into stories or categories. The resulting service was and remains a pioneer in the field of online news.

To achieve this, Adam Crozier identified 4 key goals: (i) build a world class web platform, (ii) develop all content in multi-channel format, (iii) create and own content and (iv) be first with the news. That was the task he set the organisation and every senior management meeting revolved around those 4 challenges, and as Crozier insisted "only these 4 and nothing else". Funding was raised to accelerate the organic push and acquiring content production and studios in Europe and in the US including the global leader in reality and factual shows Leftfield Entertainment. In addition, there was a major restructuring of talent and teams as well as significant all staff training to reinforce the digital and multi-channel goals.

"When we arrived a lot of people said the company was a basket case and should just be unwound, but we've been able to demonstrate just what is possible by being totally focussed on a few key objectives and only those. It meant it was easier to say no to things and not get distracted from the main aims".

4. Inject the voice of the customer

The Bupa Customer Lab: In order to drive their transformation agenda, a core initiative at the heart of new Bupa is their Customer Lab. Set up by CEO Evelyn Bourke and championed by Director John Moore, the goal here is to establish a customer-centric culture and have the voice of the customer driving decision-making.

To achieve this, they have established a number of initiatives, including setting up a team of customers who will also act as "customer reps" to constantly challenge *why are we doing things in this way, surely the customer would want it differently?* There's a group of about 20 Bupa execs working in the Customer Lab, each with specific responsibility for a key product line, a country market or line of business. The KPI include NPS scores, customer satisfaction metrics and external surveys which review how well Bupa is doing versus its competitors. These customer metrics are closely examined, reviewed constantly by the Board and are the litmus test for how well and fast the company is changing.

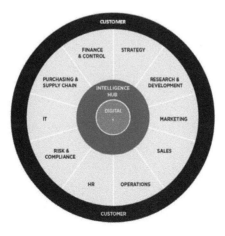

In addition, the Bupa Customer Lab team have set up an incubator to bring in new ideas, tools and applications which can help them transform the customer experience. A partnership has been forged with Microsoft and start-up ventures and small businesses are invited to pilot and test their ideas and work inside Bupa for 10 weeks with access to the company's resources and support and to develop their ideas to prototype or test. All around new ways to deliver high quality and comprehensive health, care and insurance services that can meet customers needs in the next decade.

> *"Ultimately, delivering our transformation still comes down to our people. But it's about how we talk to our customers, the customer experience we build, the brand goals we embrace and nurture, the customer life time value we can create that will make the difference."*

5. Emphasise /dramatise the urgency

Change is always easier to drive if there's a burning platform. Here's an example, albeit from some years ago but still highly relevant.

Some years ago Cadbury (before it was swallowed up by Kraft) had a biscuits /snacks business which sat alongside its core chocolate confectionery division. Often the poor cousin, the business and snacks operation suffered from lack of investment, limited product innovation and outdated manufacturing facilities. Yet its Cadbury biscuits brand name was well-loved by consumers.

After much debate, Cadbury sold its biscuits/snacks to its management team and at the time Cadbury shareholders applauded the company's commitment to its core confectionery and the focus on that.

Meantime, the MBO management team, excited by what they could achieve, faced a daunting task to revitalise the company and turn-around a heavily indebted, loss-making organisation.

The CEO of the new company was Paul Judge (who then invested in and helped establish the Cambridge University Business School) and he described the change and transformation that they then embarked on in this way:

> *"At first, it felt like we were in a sinking lifeboat, it was crisis time, water was leaking in on all sides, there was no time to discuss and debate what we should do, we were all totally united on one thing, save the boat! So it was all hands to the deck, 24/7 all single-mindedly focussed on the same goal. Looking back it was amazingly hard work, we were exhausted but it was also exhilarating as the*

boat began to stabilise, we could see we were making progress and we felt we were actually going not only to survive but to flourish.

And that is when the problems started, as soon as we had got to a solid and reasonably safe platform, we started to argue about what next! What direction should we go in, who should be responsible for what, what new equipment we should buy to start building our boat for the future? Progress started to slow. Decision-making which had taken seconds now started to take weeks. And after about 12 months, we noticed just how much things were changing.

While we had that "burning platform" things were easy, relatively. Without that we had to rethink our change programme and find new ways to energise and engage everyone in our continuing journey."

Four years after that historic management buy-out, the business was very successfully sold, but it remains a very good example of the power of "burning platforms"!

6. Agile ways of working

Much has been written about this. The key is for the organisation to trial new ways of working which can deliver more quickly. It's also about developing a mindset of "test-trial-learn".

A good example comes from Airbnb:

In an interview with the Airbnb then Head of Data Science, Riley Newman, Riley explained how the company had moved from a traditional function and often siloed way of working to adopt and embrace new Agile methods.

"We began with the usual functional teams and skill sets with their separate reporting lines but found that just encouraged siloed behaviour and no real appreciation of what might benefit the customer.

To make sure we understand the data and can capture the insights we now have core "neural" /multi-functional teams. This consists of 5 key groups: Data Scientists, Engineers, Analysts, Product Managers and Marketers. They are brought together with one team, one and the same boss, and have a joint responsibility.

"Price Tips" is example of the huge impact Agile had for us. It was one of our new features. A host can look at the calendar to see which dates are likely to be booked at their current price, as well as which aren't, and get suggestions on pricing."

Simple idea, but it took a number of learn-plan-test-measure iterations.

"Price Tips" now pulls information from billions of trading points as well as leveraging Machine Learning and personal inputs to create its data insights and to detects patterns and journeys on the web site to see why certain listings command higher prices. The goal is to be able to predict and set the optimal price.

> *"We completed this whole Price Tips solution in 8 weeks. The key was having a clear co-located, multi-discipline/multi-function team working very collaboratively together. That's the way we now approach all our projects."*

7. Break down silos.

This is a constant challenge for established organisations. How to break down years of functional, product or country-led organisation structures and develop a multi-channel collaborative integrated approach. This is also often now being described as: how do we get the organisation to have a single joined-up strategy and view of our customers, and how at the same time do we make sure the customer has a single and integrated joined-up view of us.

For years, companies felt such a goal was out of reach: "our IT systems are a mess and until we fix that, these sort of goals have to stay on the back-burner". But advances in technology with micro-services, APIs, Cloud-based solutions, the raft of emerging software tools, open source, digital eco-systems as distributed, adaptive and scalable, internet of things connectivity, mobile, data science and machine learning…all these initiatives are opening-up new possibilities to work smarter and make the sort of advances in technical competency that can make the difference.

To take advantage of these new opportunities, companies are building on Agile methods of working and now introducing "co-location". This is proving a key to break down those historic silos. Bringing people together from different parts of the company. Co-locating around the same table. No longer reporting to their functional boss but now to the Project Leader who joins them around that same table.

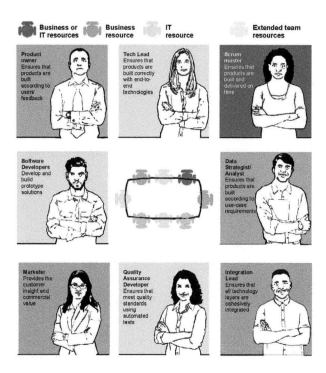

Research from Cigniti Software has shown that co-location can bring these 7 benefits:

(i) accelerates communication,

(ii) builds mutual trust and respect,

(iii) streamlines development,

(iv) enable real-time decision-making,

(v) lowers costs,

(vi) speeds up time to market

(vii) makes management easier.

As one transformation leader John Gleeson has put it: *"why not develop this approach, yes, it does require some significant organisation change in reporting lines and structure but pick one easy win short time scale project to start, prove the value and then the more widespread adoption becomes easier and easier".*

8. Town hall communications

Joe Garner, the CEO at Nationwide, is one leader who embraces open style and regular communications. Driving any change and transformation involves not just the top-down vision and strategy-setting, not just the personal commitment of the senior execs, but also of course the same level of commitment and understanding and enthusiasm of all the workforce of the company. To achieve that regular and open style communication is critical. Successful CEOs like Joe will hold many and frequent "town halls" open to everyone, an honest and unambiguous Q&A to share what's happening, why, what progress is being made, what blocks are being discovered, a call to action to everyone to get involved and help drive the progress and pace necessary.

Companies like Boots, Halfords, RWE Power, AXA, Aviva, Unilever are examples of companies who are excellent at their internal comms. They use a mix of face to face meetings, videoconference, vodcasts, CEO blogs. Bupa have their "staff happiness week", others for example establish employee reps as champions to act as advocates and department hub go-to knowledge experts (used for example by PepsiCo and IHG). O2 and ITV have also all made their mark with their level of idea sharing.

The key is to do this regularly and consistently and retain complete openness and honesty throughout. As one ITV exec put it during their major transformation journey: "those town halls were the best days of our working week".

9. Investor management

In some ways the hardest of challenges. How explain to shareholders what is happening, how gain their trust and confidence that the turnaround is truly underway, and *will* deliver, how stabilise the share price even though the benefits of the transformation have not yet come through?

There has been much talk over a number of years about investor short-termism, about the value of having a clear long term vision and strategy, about how winning companies are those that set their sights on "big hairy audacious goals" and drive the organisation to achieve them, but managing the dips and troughs that necessarily go with a transformation are now even harder to achieve with the social media spotlight exaggerating every dip and forensically examining every step of progress.

However, CEO updates and progress on restructuring can in fact lead to share price upgrades. For example, Unilever announced its long- term plans and strategic response following the take-over attempt by Kraft Heinz and even though some of the initiatives would hit the immediate bottom-line, the share price moved up 3% on expectation of a stronger future platform. Others like Barclays, BT and Aviva have all had to announce significant restructurings in recent times but won shareholder support and patience convincing that their change programmes were well-grounded and would over time deliver the benefits targeted.

McKinsey is one organisation who have been especially active and vocal about the dangers of shareholders forcing companies to take a short-term approach at the potential expense of the longer term gain. They have established their "Corporate Horizon Index". The findings show that companies on the long-term end of the spectrum dramatically outperform those classified as short term. "Among the firms we identified as focused on the long term, average revenue and earnings growth were 36 percent higher, and total return to shareholders was higher, too. The returns to society and the overall economy were equally impressive. By our measures, companies that were managed for the long term added nearly 12,000 more jobs on average than their peers over the measured 10 yr period."

While acknowledging the challenges of managing short term investor reaction, McKinsey is another voice seeking to encourage longer term planning, business development and shareholder management.

10. Link pay and benefits

To some extent this "key to transformation success" is obvious and the benefits of linking exec pay to delivery of the key business goals is clear.

The challenge is to ensure that the targets and goals are very directly connected to the transformation agenda and that each person on the team is indeed given measurable targets that they personally can act on and feel accountable for. In some instances pay and benefits is simply linked to "good performance" at the discretion of the line manager and perhaps without the clear transformation target-setting.

Research from Willis Towers Watson found that: "employees are struggling to see the link between pay and performance at their workplaces. The Workforce Study found that only a minority of workers (37%) see a clear link between their pay and performance. Less than half (46%) said they thought that their company does a good job explaining its pay programmes. Only four in 10 (40%) felt that their manager makes fair decisions on how their performance links to pay awards.

But the study also found that the lack of connection between pay and performance is becoming less common now as the need to transform is starting to affect and impact most every organisation, forcing managers to focus ever more closely on key target delivery. As the Willis Towers Watson survey concluded: "it will be important for companies to get this right, as reward will be an ever more critical tool in encouraging employees to go the extra mile in delivering their company's transformation targets".

★★★★★

Business transformation has of course never been easy; changing sometimes decades of working practices, processes and structures, trying to inculcate a mindset which accepts and even embraces the need for change, explaining the role and impact that technology advances are having and winning hearts and minds support for the necessary new strategies and direction the company must take. As the Cadbury /Premier Brands example shows, having a sense of urgency, even crisis, can help as a catalyst, but to really build a sustainable and long-term platform for future success then all 10 of these key lessons learned need to be aligned and in place and worked on to enable the transformation to happen.

To sum up in the words of Wal-Mart CEO Doug McMillon: "we have embarked on a long term journey to change this corporation…we are making a massive investment in digital transformation…we have to move from stores-based to omni-channel…we're training the whole workforce, all our associates to build a stronger foundation…we're learning that we can and need to partner with others to accelerate our progress (acquisitions of eg e-commerce Jet. com and logistics start-up Parcel)…we need to reboot our whole approach to customer data and personalisation…we have to take on the Amazon.com juggernaut…with our now deep commitment to change we are going to unlock the huge potential we have to succeed in the digital age".

Chapter 8

What is the HR impact of
digital on future talent needs and hiring?

Digital
Transformation
and HR

To what extent is digital changing the type of candidate that organisations are looking for? Has the arrival of this digital technology and multi-channel world changed the underlying characteristics and attributes of a successful modern-day hire? Have we reached a sea-change in the type of skills, attitude and outlook that it takes to succeed?

Certainly, right now there is a wide-spread view that it is hard to find good "digital" people. In a survey by e-Consultancy, 68% of HR professionals said they had difficulty recruiting staff who were sufficiently knowledgeable about digital technology and communications. 73% commented that digital was making a significant impact on preferred candidate profiles and 43% commented on the challenge of keeping up to date with the new digital trends and tools. What's more HR teams are having themselves to become increasingly "digitally savvy". 74% said they had had to become more skilled in using online search tools to find out about a candidate's reputation and 46% said they had rejected a candidate based on what they had discovered about a person online with Facebook, YouTube and blogs being cited as key influences.

So "Digital" is making a substantial impact in the way companies generally do organise and go to market. A recent study by BCG (Boston Consulting

Group) together with Google showed that the "digital economy" is already making a significant contribution to US and UK GDP, eg worth more than 7% of UK GDP at more than £100bn. That makes it larger than the construction, utilities and transportation sectors! And it is fast growing, expected to double over the next 5 years. At that level it will be larger than the Financial Services sector!

"Digital" is now a widely used term and it has become a catch-all umbrella for a whole range of different skills and requirements. For example, within "digital marketing" there are a large number of specialist skills. These include: Search engine marketing, search engine optimisation, affiliate marketing, web analytics, campaign analysis, creative marketing, brand strategy development, customer retention, eCRM, email marketing, and now add on mobile commerce, social media and interactive TV. All these areas are unique and distinctive skill sets. They all require a candidate with specific know-how and skills. But if a business team asks for a "digital marketeer", there is often the assumption that someone with knowledge of the online world can turn their hand to any and all of these very different things. And yet what can make a difference is a candidate who really is for example, steeped and immersed in mobile, or in social media, who really does have the case studies and the war stories and the lessons learnt so that they know intuitively what will drive successful comms, content and commerce.

The same can be said for the technology area. In a recent survey by IBM of 2000 IT professionals, 91% said that digital technology tools would dominate and would form the primary IT delivery model. They mentioned a wide range of skill set requirements from IT visioning and enterprise architecture, through to SOA (service-oriented architecture) and SaaS (software as a service) and Cloud computing. The IT community are also placing a much higher emphasis on Programme Management and delivery, recognising that the migration to a new digital technology environment will likely need transformational change across geography and business units and will need expert tech and commercial change and delivery skills. There are also core and specialist skill requirements around IT infrastructure, Cloud, data centres, data protection and security, MIS (management information services), social networks, mobile, voice recognition, content management, "green IT" and the multitude of different software programming skills from Dot Net to Java to Open Source experience to HTML5 and so on....

It's a challenging environment, it's new and there are no real proven solutions. Businesses are forced to learn and experiment as they go and make a bet, however reasoned, on what are the core skills and needs to help drive the future success and growth of the organisation. And that is often why job specs for "digital" jobs are difficult to write. Unlike for example a search for a new financial controller where there are many years of understanding and experience as to the sort of qualifications and experience required. Digital expertise is harder to define and describe. What are the right qualifications, what sort of university degree is most relevant, how evaluate years of hands-on experience, how valuable is someone who is steeped in IT generally versus a new grad who has grown up using and learning the new digital tools and environment? If there's a need for a marketer, then how transferable are for example search engine marketing skills into a more general online marketing remit? If looking for a new architect how familiar and expert do they need to be for example in cloud computing, if according to IBM, that will be a specific area that will dominate IT development?

In summary, there are probably 5 key things that can be identified from all the research and experience that distinguish a candidate who is best-suited for the digital world. The focus here is less on the specific skills eg in Search engine marketing specialisation or in SOA, but more around the qualitative attributes that mark out an individual. What is the "right stuff" that HR teams and business owners should be looking for? It's all changing so fast and hard to know what will be required in the business in 12 months' time, let alone 3 years out. But can we put together a simple and sustainable check-list of core attributes and characteristics?

The 5 keys are:

1. *A restless spirit*
2. *Comfort and confident with technology (but not necessarily a "techie")*
3. *Communication and interpersonal skills*
4. *Self-sufficiency*
5. *An appreciation that it's a multi-channel world*

A restless spirit: this is someone who enjoys and relishes change! It's the individual who is happy that there is no complete job spec, who is comfortable that there is no clearly defined box for the role, it's that person who recognises that we are going through a revolution in communications and in technology and who wants to be part of that, contributing to it, challenging traditions and accepted methodologies and processes, a force for change who is unhappy if things are status quo or if things take too long to happen, an inquisitive mind who wants to know about the latest technologies and tools and is passionate about them.

Comfort and confident with technology: this is a vital prerequisite. They need not necessarily have a deep tech background if they are for example up for a marketing role, but they must have an appreciation of it, a desire to understand it and ability to talk about it. They need to know what is "cloud computing", why it's being so widely discussed and be able to see the potential commercial applications. They need to appreciate that doing something in mobile for example is not just about "creating an app for the iPhone" but that there are scores of other handsets which need to be separately managed and that configuration of the online site may require significant technical resource. They need to be a point of contact that can translate tech advances into commercial feasibility

Communication and Interpersonal skills: a recent survey by the US Center for Public Education highlighted this area as a key requirement. "The 21st Century is bringing a requirement for new skills and tools in the workspace. Strong interpersonal skills for collaboration and communication will be a "must-have" competency. It's the power to interact effectively, to communicate both face-to-face, in large and small meetings, both verbally and with data, to relate well to others and to cooperate with them, to negotiate and manage potential conflicts of priority between departments and to lead through persuasion. In times of change and especially where organisations are having to adopt new technologies and new ways of working, this is going to be a core skill".

Self sufficiency: organisations are already moving toward remote working environments. The concept of everyone travelling to an office to do a day's work and do that every day of the week is a not a 21st century way of working. Unilever for example have adopted a workplace strategy which looks at three categories of employee. They call it "resident, mobile and offsite". Residents are still those who come to work and have their own desk and workspace. That might be eg the office manager, security staff as well as others who prefer that style. The Mobile worker has typically been the salesperson out and about with customers but returning to base and hot-desking there, so having access but no "permanent home". And then the Remote worker, who may never visit the office, may be established at home or be a connected contractor or consultant or supplier who needs and gets access to fellow employees, office news and information, email etc but mostly from a remote station.

Unilever are also studying how the next 5 years will further change that categorisation. One thing they are certain about: there will still be a need for an office, but there will be a substantial shift from resident to mobile and offsite. This has far-reaching impact on people. Are they the sort that can cope with this change in work pattern? Are they self-sufficient in that they could be set up to eg work from home? Are they reliable in that they may have limited physical contact with colleagues and it will be harder to monitor their performance?

Appreciation it's a multi-channel world: while this has all been about digital, it is just as important for good candidates to appreciate that there is a much that is not digital. 20% of the UK population are not online, e-commerce accounts for some 15% to 20% plus of total retail and while many will research online, still the majority will shop and buy in-store. TV advertising still accounts for some 40% of all advertising spend and is still the key way for any organisation wishing to build a mass wide-reaching consumer brand. 78% of consumers have smart phones with Net access but that still means a significant number that do not and most people today will shop and research and interact in a multi-channel and cross platform way. So it's critical that good marketers and technology people do appreciate this, do understand that you can't just "switch off analogue" overnight, that the spread of online and digital technology will still be unfolding and that any business solution will need to accommodate customers wherever they are and through whatever channel they choose to interact.

★★★★★

It's always been a challenge of course to find the best candidates for the organisation. There will always be competition for the very best people and a premium on their time and services. But as we look at the next few years it is clear that digital is placing an added layer of complexity. There is more demand than supply for the best talent and that puts a bigger emphasis on the 5 keys discussed here: to find those individuals with the spirit, the confidence, the interpersonal skills, the self-sufficiency and the strategic multi-channel awareness that they can operate effectively in this digital world and make the outstanding impact that they've been hired for.

Chapter 9

Employee engagement is the key to digital change and transformation

In these transformation times, when Digital & Data Tech are driving so much change and opportunity, what can make the difference in achieving success? What key factors are emerging that show how winning companies can succeed, how the various challenges with delivering change can be met and overcome, how an organisation can develop to be a Digital & Data winner.

The research is showing that a key driver is *Employee Engagement*. It's about enabling and mobilising and empowering and exciting the workforce to engage wholeheartedly with the transformation programme, to get involved in it with enthusiasm, instilling a belief that this effort and their personal contribution can lead to success.

Companies like 3M, Zappos, Virgin, Red Hat, Nationwide Building Society, LV Insurance, Adobe, Home Depot, Procter & Gamble, South West Airlines and others are leading the way in this respect. They are showing that:

Employee Engagement = Customer Happiness = Market Success.

Let's look at some initial stats around this whole area:

- Sasser & Reichheld at Harvard Business School found that "employee engagement" was the key to driving customer satisfaction and hence market success. Their research showed that through employee engagement, if that drove a 5% increase in customer loyalty then that could increase profits in the company by as much as 25%.

- McKinsey found that c.70% of all customer buying decisions are based on how well they are treated by the organisation and its employees
- Gallup Consulting discovered that high employee engagement companies grow their earnings per share ("EPS") at a faster rate of 28% while low employee engagement firms experienced an average EPS decline rate of 9.4%.
- The Center for Human Resources Strategy at Rutgers University found that businesses with highly engaged workforces were on average 3.4x more effective financially in terms of sales and revenue growth

We can also consider some overview case study examples:

Virgin: "At Virgin, we do not put the customer first. It's Virgin employees who are the company's top priority. That may sound like a decades-old business wisdom, but it works. If the person who works at your company is 100 per cent proud of the Brand and you give them a good job and they're treated well, they're going to be happy and they're going to make the customers pleased too"

-interview with Richard Branson

Red Hat: "I have never seen a company of this size where the people are so passionate"

-quote from annual CIO.com customer survey

Zappos: "We hire talent whose personal values align with the company's core values. Our employees are encouraged to have a genuine interest in helping others. We're proud that they say they feel inspired. They say they are able to fulfil a higher personal purpose at work by being enabled to live out their own values very day. Great benefits and a workplace that is fun and dedicated to making customers happy all fit in with the Zappos approach to company culture – when you get the company culture right, great customer service and a great Brand will happen on its own. Change becomes easy!"

Gary Hamel: Business School Professor: "To put it bluntly, the most important task for any manager today is to create a work environment that inspires exceptional contribution and that merits an outpouring of passion, imagination and initiative".

Southwest Airlines: "We've been in operation for more than 50 years and during all that time we have looked to communicate our goals and vision to our employees in a way that will make them feel part here of a unified team. We want our people to be convinced of a larger common goal and to be excited by that. In that way we believe they will feel empowered to go the extra mile to make our customers happy"

These case studies and research show that there is a key underlying model at work underpinning this employee engagement success. It's not just nice words, it's not simply some top-down statement of intent, it's not simply yet another initiative to try to build-up the company. It is something much more fundamental, that's root and branch and becomes the DNA as to how people think, work and collaborate across the organisation:

The Employee Engagement Model

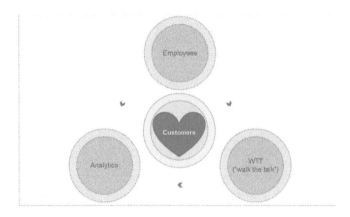

We can look in more detail and specifically at how 3 companies live and breathe this employee engagement model: Nationwide Building Society, LV Insurance and South West Airlines

Nationwide

Nationwide has over 15 millions members/customers across the UK. It is the second largest UK Bank in terms of consumer savings and mortgages with assets of more than £200bn.

It has consistently been ranked among in the top 5 best big companies to work for, has been voted No.1 UK Bank by Business Insider, has been the Which? Banking Brand of the Year and described in a consumer survey as: "the most trustworthy, straightforward, helpful and friendly Bank" (Good Housekeeping).

Joe Garner, an ex P&G person, is the CEO there. He talks in this way about how Nationwide is organised and managing continuous change:

"We have a mission to build a trusted community of customers and employees…customers stay with us because of our record of outstanding customer services… that's being given every day by our staff and it is at the heart of what we do.

"Underpinning our success is our recognition of our employees. There is a sense of Pride that runs through the whole organisation so that our employees want to serve our customers in the best possible way.

Nationwide has established a range of employee benefits which include time off for local charity volunteer work, everyone eligible for the pension scheme and a minimum 4% employer contribution, free healthcare for employees and their family, flexible working including part time, flexi time, school term time only and home /remote working, minimum 24 days holiday for all, vouchers /employee rewards each week for work well-done, celebrations of employees "who go the extra mile" with their stories published for all to read, long service awards…employees feel valued and their efforts recognised.

Supporting this are detailed customer analytics. There's a substantial investment in understanding the key customer metrics, what is working and what is not and at a detailed level by branch, by department, by team so that good performance can be immediately identified and any areas needing improvement can quickly get attention. The data available is increasingly in real-time so no need to wait for a report to come through from IT at the end of a month or quarter, the areas of opportunity are easily visible.

And as the key that keeps all these good things in place, Joe Garner is a very good example of a business leader who walks the talk. Joe talks about the "courage to care" (and see later chapter), the desire to do the right thing by staff and customers, the goal of building a caring environment where staff can flourish and change can be delivered. He cascades these messages throughout the organisation all the time. He also holds regular "town hall" meetings where progress is shared and success celebrated. "There's a level of openness and transparency at Nationwide that I've not seen anywhere else" -employee comments on glassdoor.co.uk).

LV Insurance

LV is one of the UK's largest insurance companies with more than 5 million customers and offering a range of personal and life insurance, pension and savings.

It has been voted "best loved insurer" 5 yrs running, it has been rated by Moneywise as "most trusted insurer" and has won best life and pensions provider 8x by Moneyfacts.

CEO Richard Rowney talks in these terms: "Our goal is to help customers, members and colleagues feel more confident about life and more confident in us. We have a strong customer service ethos. They are at the centre of what we do. We know we have to keep evolving and improving and taking advantage of new technologies in a way that's helpful to us and to our customers and not to replace the tried and tested. Companies like Amazon and John Lewis set the bar for what customers expect and we need to keep investing and building. So we are always trying to improve our employee experience, *recognising that great customer experience starts from the inside out."*

Like Nationwide, LV too have a generous array of employee benefits to help their staff engage. Everyone is eligible for the LV bonus scheme, all are able to participate in the pension plan up to a 14% matched contribution, there are coffee cards for new joiners, healthcare, holidays for top-performing employees and their families, weekly thank you cards and gift vouchers with more than 23,000 sent out in the last year (workforce of 5000), flexible working, crowdsourcing/funding plans for new ideas, a customer leadership academy…a lot of effort going in to make employees feel valued and motivated.

LV also have underpinned these efforts with a detailed customer analytics capability that continuously measures customer and employee engagement. As their Head of Analytics points out:

"we are now able to analyse the experience of our customers at a collective as well as at an individual level so that we can continue to shape and improve that experience. We can engage in real-time 1-1 as well as identifying an ongoing programme of change and improvement".

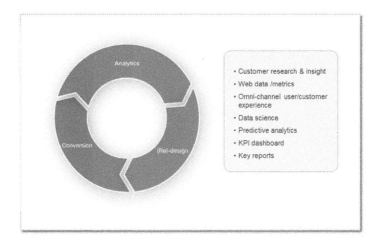

Richard Rowney is also a keen advocate of "walking the talk". He talks about wanting to: "build the culture to make everybody around feel welcome and looking to help each other. We like to encourage that especially. There's lots of communication at LV as well and I expect all my mangers to be out there walking around talking to people. We care here about our staff and members and it can be seen constantly".

South West Airlines

Founded in 1967, SWA has become the largest domestic US airline. Revenues exceed \$21bn. They have now recorded their 45th consecutive year of profitability (while some once rival carriers have either merged or reported continued trading difficulties). The share price is up 3x over the past 5yrs.

SWA has been named for the 24th straight year as one of Forbes Most Admired Companies. They are consistently ranked No. 1 Airline for customer satisfaction, have been voted "one of the best employers to work for" in glassdoor polls for the 9th year running, named in the top 100 for Corporate Responsibility and voted best US Airline for 8 consecutive years.

This is a company that completely subscribes to the mantra that employee engagement drives customer satisfaction = market success. In the company's annual report, the first thing that CEO Gary Kelly says is: "I want to thank our people for our exceptional results and congratulate them. Our strong financial performance provides the cash flow to continue to reward our employees…and so deliver more value to our customers". SWA announced it would share \$586m of its profits with its 54,000 workforce, making an average bonus payout of 13.2% or the equivalent of 6 weeks pay.

"*Our people-first approach* has guided our company since it was founded and it means when our company does well, our people do really, really well. Our people work incredibly hard and deserve to share in Southwest's success."

As pointed out in a recent Forbes review of the company, SWA has never laid anyone off or cut pay. They have long been lauded for their strong workplace culture and engaged workforce. They work hard to get employees to think and act like owners and by sharing the profits they are able to make a substantial statement of intent. "The real secret to Southwest's success is having one of the most highly motivated and productive work forces in the world. They are motivated by a sense of fairness that says: *We want your well-being [as an employee] to be tied to the company's well-being because, after all, you are the company.*"

For SWA, analytics has also always been a key part of how they manage and measure performance. They have been described as a "big data company" long before IBM pioneered big data teams. And the aim of investment and building the analytics capability has always been around improving and delivering the highest quality of customer service.

The goal today is to establish a "self-serve" analytics culture enabling employees to get information themselves in real-time and so be able to respond immediately. So front-line personnel receive real-time KPI dashboards related to operational and strategic goals. They can use voice commands to eg extract information out of live-recorded interactions between customers and staff. They can monitor and review social media data to check on performance and what customers are saying and intervene immediately to fix an issue or capture a customer booking. The whole purpose is to drive higher customer conversion through employees able and willing and wanting to make a positive impact and contribution (and being rewarded accordingly).

"Walk the Talk" is another key part of the SWA success story. It was part of founder Herb Kelleher's DNA and that has been picked up with enthusiasm by successive management teams. For example, each and every quarter, all execs spend a full day doing the job of a frontline employee. It could be as check-in attendant, clean-up crew or baggage handler, and with the aim of making sure that all the workforce in every department know what customers are saying and what best customer service looks like. It's a detailed and deliberate program with the aim of leaving no stone unturned.

CEO Gary Kelly sums up in this way: "I am committed to spending my time on our culture and taking care of our people. It is a focus and mindset and our highest priority, we walk the talk."

★★★★★

Building a culture of employee engagement is not easy. GE for example embarked some years ago on a company-wide training programme investing many millions in training their entire workforce of more than 300,000 worldwide operating in everything from Oil & Gas to Financing to Computing. It was set-up as a key initiative by then CEO Jeff Immelt to immerse everyone in digital and help understand the need for change and the opportunities it could bring. The aim was to get everyone ready and eager for the planned digital transformation of the corporation.

But the training did not achieve the desired results. Often it was poorly delivered, outsourced to many different providers, not tailored to local needs or local business issues, it was not well attended and perhaps only lasted a half day. It wasn't enough. It was the kind of traditional top-down initiative which looked good on a Board paper but didn't strike at the heart of what was needed. It did not motivate and as some said it in fact "pretty much demotivated everyone here".

Companies talk eagerly about "it's people who make the difference". But often that mantra trips off the tongue without being clearly understood, lost amid an array of other initiatives and priorities, relegated to an occasional hour of time or quarterly review, it cannot make an impact.

As we can see from the case examples described here, it requires a very determined effort. It does mean asking some very far-reaching questions: do we put our employees first, how would they rate and review that, what should we be doing to drive that, what kind of investment in time and energy will it take, are we willing and ready to *truly* do that, do we believe in our hearts that it will pay back, do we believe it will be the foundation of a winning formula and lasting sustainable and renewable success?

Chapter 10

How measure employee engagement

How measure employee engagement, how do we know if the efforts and investments in the workforce are paying back, how to understand which actions are working and which not and where to focus future energies?

It's all about developing the key metrics and KPi, establishing the dashboard and critically monitoring that over time to see what progress is being made. And that monitoring needs to be done frequently, the best organisations are now doing it in real time, so that success can be seen and any need to intervene can be immediately identified.

The VW Group in Australia provides a good initial example. Knowing that engaged employees are a huge driver of customer advocacy, they needed a platform that would enable them to measure and improve the customer experience and especially the role employees could play in delivering that.

Volkswagen used to monitor the customer experience, but the insights they were collecting weren't timely enough to be useful for employees at their 104 dealerships. Insights were often being shared with dealer employees 3-4 months after they had been collected—if they were being shared at all. As a result, the insights weren't inspiring action. Employees needed real-time experience data in order to learn and improve.

VW invested in a new technology solution with software partner Qualtrics to collect and distribute insights in real-time, and to establish dashboards that could deliver actionable insights. They quickly found that the top 10 dealers with the best employee engagement and retention scores, they were having the best and most consistent set of customer sales. The most engaged employees were perhaps not surprisingly getting the best results and had the largest proportion of customers who spoke highly about the dealership and the Brand.

This led VW to completely revamp their employee engagement efforts. *Build success through the employee.* The aim was to encourage employees to take pride in delivering an exceptional customer experience. Training and reward programmes were set up. Customer service metrics were published. All the dealerships reoriented their structure to an "employee-first" culture. And customers responded. It has led to a significant increase in repeat purchasing, loyalty and advocacy.

Importantly, employees were not just encouraged to take pride and go the extra mile but they were rewarded to. It all can become a self-fulfilling cycle.

In order to measure employee engagement, it's important to start by understanding the broader market context:

- *60% of employees say there are mechanisms in place to provide employee feedback and comments. But only 30% say that feedback is ever followed up by the employer*
  -Deloitte

- *According to Qualtrics research, average employee engagement levels are at 62% in the US, 48% in the UK and 56% in Australia*

- *only 40% of the workforce report that they know and understand what are the company's goals and strategies and so why they are doing the job they are asked to do.*
  -Bain Consulting

- *...but "highly engaged" employees are 87% less likely to leave their companies*
  -Corporate Leadership Council

- *and every 1% increase in employee engagement can deliver a 0.6% increase in revenue on a sustainable basis*
  -Peakon and Hays Group research

- *Highly engaged companies have 37% fewer sick days, 30% higher productivity levels and 2.5x better customer satisfaction scores*
  -Peakon and Hays

- *Such "highly engaged" companies average 58% lower churn costs which can save huge amounts in having to find, recruit, onboard and get new replacements up-to-speed.*
-Peakon and Hays

The optimal solution is clearly to maximise employee retention, as the longer someone is in the company, the more they know, the quicker they can work as they are familiar with the key processes and systems, the more efficient and so productive they can be, the better they can build cross-department and cross-company relationships so they can easily fix a problem or make a team decision, and the better they know the customer base and individual customers and what they need, and what they do not, and so how best to win new business and secure customer trust and confidence. There's nothing better than hearing the expression: "we've always worked with ABC Co, they know us, they've never let us down, yes, there are competitors but why change when we know we'll get what we want when we want it".

There are a number of employee engagement measurement systems that can be deployed. The most popular is Net Promoter Score otherwise known as Employee or eNPS and this has been adopted by many large corporations in the USA and is becoming increasingly used in Europe and Asia.

In the early 1990's Fred Reichheld, a researcher at Bain & Co consulting led a research project to find the most efficient way to measure customer satisfaction. He found that traditional surveys took too long and ended up drowning in data "it's always possible to find some positive spin if there's enough data to play with". So Reichheld asked: what would be the one key question you need to ask to establish levels of customer loyalty. And the simple solution question he came up with is: How likely is it that you would recommend ABC Co to a friend or colleague? Reichheld also suggested a simple scoring out of 10 where 10 would be the most positive response.

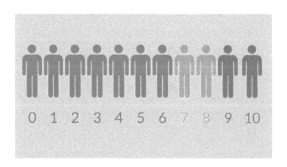

Reichheld then went on to give another dimension to this scoring by grouping the answers into 3 categories:

- *Promoters*: give the score 9 or 10 and are "extremely likely" to recommend
- *Passively Satisfied*: they give a score of 7 or 8 and are neutral. They're not likely to recommend but they're satisfied with the service
- *Detractors*: give a score of 0 to 6 and are not all likely to recommend.

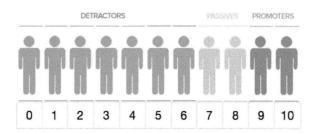

One of the early adopters of the Reichheld NPS method was Apple. They started using it in their stores to identify their best employees: which employees were having the best impact with customers and what were they doing that was special, what could be learned therefore that could be passed on to other employees and what in fact could be enshrined as best practice and shown and taught to the whole workforce, from Day 1, when they joined, so they'd know from the get-go what to do, how to do it, what behaviours worked best and so maximise the impact for each and every single customer.

And easy to start by having this one simple measure that could be asked of all customers.

Over time, companies like Apple have systematically adopted this NPS approach to see if the total efforts of the organisation were working for its employees too. And so they adapted the question and developed the eNPS scoring.

"On a scale of 0 to 10, how likely is it that you would recommend this company as a place to work?"

Of course the scoring is all very well, but the key is and real value comes in the follow-ups. The learning around the scoring is that it can change and change quickly. A "Promoter" today with a 9 or even a 10 score can quickly become a detractor if the company changes materially in how it operates or behaves towards its staff. So these scores need a regular monitor and check.

Equally if someone is a "Detractor" today, then important to understand why is that: "what is the key thing that's stopping you promoting the company, what's holding you back, what needs to change?

Companies have been encouraged to calculate a net eNPS score:

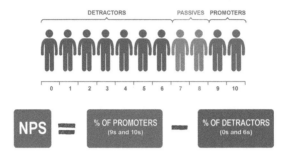

This can mean that a company's eNPS score can be negative. For example, if 30% promote but 40% detract then the score is -10.

Reichheld's research showed that people who give scores of 7 or 8 were not to be included as follow-up surveys showed they were typically neutral and not likely to go one way or the other.

The key question then becomes what is a good eNPS score? The score can vary anywhere from -100 to + 100. What's been found over time is that realistically getting a positive score is good and anything from +10 to +30 is already a score to be proud of. Employees are usually tough critics and are so very invested in their work and the organisation they're part of, so that they have been found to give out top scores more sparingly. It's also the case that US employees are typically more ready to give positive and enthusiastic scores especially in comparison to European employees who are found to be slightly more conservative and cautious in their appraisal.

Comparably.com now offers a very comprehensive view of a company's eNPS score and it is also possible to compare and contrast with rivals in the same industry sector.

Just type in the company name. There is a wealth of data there on each organisation,

For example they have developed their own "company culture" score:

- Overall company culture scores vary from A+ to D-
- Key culture dimensions which are each separately scored on an A+ to D- range looking at: Office culture, diversity, retention rates, how good are the Exec team, workplace environment, perks & benefits and professional development

- employees can rate their co-worker as well as the Leadership team and the CEO specifically
- reviews about working at the company
- and the overall eNPS score calculated by Comparably.com from those who have visited their web site and contributed to their survey and key questions.

What we can see immediately is that those companies that are generally perceived in the marketplace to be good places to work do get very good scores.

- Apple has an eNPS of +25
- Adobe, one of todays' generally highest rated companies, has a +56 eNPS
- South West Airlines, another favourite, scores at +52
- LEGO is at +24
- Prudential USA +49
- Tesla +43

On the other hand:

- American Airlines is -10
- Target is 2
- Walmart is -11
- Cognizant is -14
- Western Union is -25
- Elsevier is -33
- Deutsche Bank -50

Identifying and being aware of how employees regard the company should be among the most critical KPI. Yet it is often something that is not measured carefully or perhaps only once a year, and often the scoring is buried in an organisation development team with a report that only has limited circulation. Yet some measures can quickly be found at no cost, such as looking at employee feedback score on Glassdoor or on Indeed.com or at Comparably.com. And for those companies that do look at these widely publicly available feedback reviews, they may see a score of 3 out 5 and say that's ok, we're at the average, we're doing alright, no red alerts. But as we have seen from the Reichheld eNPS system, mid-level scores, the 6s and the 7s count for little. Such average scores do not indicate there is a group of "promoters" out there who will be your ambassadors and who will promote your organisation and advertise its values and encourage other good employees to join or help persuade prospective customers that this is *the best place to do business*.

And therein lies the challenge. Most companies pay lip service to the idea of employee engagement. Few think through: what will it take to get to a 9 or 10 eNPS or a 4 or 5 on Glassdoor or a retention rate of more than 90%?

Employees can make the difference. Customer service from a chatbot may be adequate, it can do its job efficiently. But it cannot by definition innovate and act out of the box and go the extra mile and get that extra level of customer satisfaction. That is the difference motivated employees can make.

Chapter 11

Winning in the talent wars

-the new 1-week paradigm

Why do the GAFA (Google, Apple, Facebook and Amazon) companies seem to always get the best talent? Is it just because they've got strong Brand names, is it because they pay more or is it something much more straightforward that any company could replicate? Is there a "secret to their success" that other companies can learn from and embrace?

This chapter sets out the answer and it all comes down to the new paradigm in the talent wars game. It's about using Agile methods to win. Managing a recruiting process that is done simultaneously, not in waterfall. Prioritising, galvanising teams, setting short time lines, having clear goals -day by day (not month by month): establishing a new *1-week paradigm.*

It's the idea of moving very fast once top talent is identified. It's about building a momentum and excitement which sweeps the candidate off their feet. It's about a mindset which has the same laser focus as winning a big new customer order. Some call it "closing the deal". How can we harness and coordinate *all our resources* to land the win, how do we ensure we beat out the competition and make us the preferred option? Yes, we have to be in a good state revenue and profit-wide, yes, we need to show growth and career prospects, yes we need to have a clearly defined role and remit and set of responsibilities, yes, the pay and benefits needs to be competitive, but what's the key to unlock all that potential and get the best talent on-board?

What's this new *1-week paradigm*? It's about: organising so that once the key talent is identified, then line up the interviews and move to offer *within one week*. Overwhelm the candidate with interest, positivity and enthusiasm. Make the whole thing exciting. Use the one week to show "we can move fast" in this new tech-driven /digital world, we can be as smart as anyone and this demonstrates we really want you.

There's been many books written about "competitive advantage through people", showcasing case studies that demonstrate that people are the key assets of the organisation, that through people the company can win if the workforce is motivated and properly managed. Some companies will talk about being customer-centric and being customer-led. But the more savvy will talk about "power through people", they will see the virtuous circle that if their employees are motivated and excited and informed and care about what the company is doing, then that will naturally translate through to the way they connect and engage with customers and through that they will drive market success and advantage. In the UK, leading retailer John Lewis is probably the best example of that where all its staff are called partners and all share in the profits of the company and where there is a constant cascade of values and ideals about equality and togetherness and feeling part of the company's mission and purpose. Others like Next plc, Estee Lauder, Nationwide, Admiral Insurance, even the likes of Accenture and Deloitte are all scored highly by employees as best places to work.

So if people are the key, then not surprising that there's an ongoing war for the best, and not surprising that GAFA companies, being new to set up, have been able to adopt and embrace a best practice approach from day 1.

We all read nowadays about how companies should become more agile, how they should move from linear thinking to agile ways of working, So GAFA have embraced that ideal in their talent acquisition process. It's not any more about let's set up the first interview, see how that goes, then set up the next one, and then after that let's do another. Now instead, the process is as follows:

- *Day 1 Monday*: meet a top talent for the first time, if like what you meet.
- *Day 2: Tuesday:* call first thing, invite back in
- *Day 3: Wednesday*: line up 5 interviews all on the same day
- *Day 4: Thursday*: **make offer**, invite to come in /meet the team, send contract by email end of day
- *Day 5 Friday*: end of day drinks with all the interviewers, **shake hands, sign.**

Day 5 is "close the deal day". What do we have to do to get this person on-board? Let's see if we can capture the week's momentum, let's keep the buzz, nothing more powerful than having this person back with us, offer letter on the table, a "signing ceremony", it doesn't have to be done shyly and privately behind closed doors, let's imagine it's like a star footballer signing their new contract in front of the world's press and photographers. We can make a show of it and in doing so show how much we want this person to join.

And yes, the offer letter can be subject to references and contain 3-month probation clauses to give the company added security and safeguard but in principle we all want to go home Friday evening with the deal closed, the job done, this brilliant new talent signed-up.

★★★★★

Why don't all companies operate in this way? Why do many especially large organisations take months and months to go through a process of interviews and consideration? Is it any wonder that such companies with such a process may lose out on the best?

In recent times I have seen in my recruitment work a step-change in the level of interest and demand for example in Data, Analytics and Insight roles. Whether as Chief Data Officer, or Director of Analytics, or Head of Insight, companies all now can see the value that good data management can bring to underpin more effective customer and pricing decision-making.

As an example, one recent client of mine is a FTSE 100 Financial Services organisation. They created a new role which was to be their Chief Data Officer. The role was seen as important enough for the organisation that it would it report direct to the CEO and potentially could become a main Board position.

The company had talked about the need for urgency, they recognised there is a lot of demand for the best talent in this space, how it was imperative to move quickly, how this would be a high profile appointment for the company and so important to get the best.

A shortlist of candidates, identified, checked and ready to meet was completed in less than 3 weeks. This is what the company did next:

- Week 1: meet the shortlist of candidates
- Week 2: evaluate and consider and review feedback internally
- Week 3: identify top 3 to move forward with
- Week 4: get back with next step dates /meeting options for 2 weeks' time
- Week 6: second-round interviews
- Week 7: review internal feedback
- Week 8: decide on top 2 to move forward with
- Week 10: third-round interviews

…and so on…with final interview at the end of 3 months.

Guess what happened? The final candidate gets an offer from the client but that same week they get approached by a GAFA company.

One week later candidate has a new offer to consider, and it's exciting. "these guys moved really quickly, they really showed they wanted me, they're putting quite a lot of pressure on me to accept this week, I've been invited back in later today for a drinks /more informal meeting with the interviewers, I'll let you know how that goes…

In the end the company did get their person. But it was touch and go for a couple of weeks while the candidate was getting to know a new quick Agile and fast-moving company and comparing that with the slower more traditional pace and wondering what that said about the two companies and ways of working and potential at each.

The good news is that not only did the client company eventually win-out but they also wanted to learn and understand what it was that the GAFA company was doing and how was it able to move so quickly.

The company has now established a new "top talent" interview process". They felt that adopting the 1-week paradigm was at this stage perhaps too big a jump for them. But what about 1-month? It would not be the fastest but it would represent a step-change in their speed and agility and in doing so give the company a much better of chance of securing the top talent it wanted in the future.

To underpin that a new dashboard was established which would help the HR and Talent Acquisition teams to measure and monitor how efficiently they were able to manage the recruitment process:

- *Time from brief to offer*
- *Time from first interview to offer*
- *Time from offer to close*
- *Number of interviews*
- *% of interviews on same day*
- *% offers accepted*

★★★★★

What can recruiters and headhunters do to facilitate this? One easy solution is to speed up their own process. It's no longer acceptable to spend 2 or 3 weeks indulging in "mapping the market" and then another 3 or 4 weeks while the recruiting firm trawls that market. That can mean 6 weeks or more from brief before the company even sees sight of an early shortlist.

This new "1-week paradigm" requires a fast approach from the off. In my recruiting work, I commit to get the shortlist within 2 to 3 weeks maximum. I don't waste time briefing junior researchers, I am able to leverage many yrs personal experience and networks and get straight to potential candidates on day 1 after the brief. By the end of week 1, I can already have the start of the shortlist ready to go. All that means momentum, speed and agility and the ability to get the process up and running very quickly. I'm finding that can make a significant difference as I only work on one role at a time, so all my efforts and energies are dedicated to getting to the best candidates and getting them excited and ready to interview.

★★★★★

In today's fast-moving world, no process can be complete and no new ways of working can guarantee success. But it's clear that to capture the best talent in the market, companies do have to learn to move more quickly, to develop that GAFA-like buzz and excitement with the candidate that ensures they are keen and ready to sign-up and join. It can come down to the simple process changes described here that any organisation can adopt and give itself the best chance of success.

Chapter 12

Using the recruitment process to benchmark candidates and resolve uncertainty

There are many studies now pointing to a shortage of Digital and Data skills, more demand than quality supply, as companies race to find and build the best talent pools and teams. With the war for talent getting ever more competitive, so companies are having to become more flexible in the way they consider recruiting and the speed that they move ahead.

A recent Gartner survey pointed out that one of the common roadblocks which gets in the way of quickly and effectively building digital and data teams is "uncertainty". They found that execs often delay because they are unsure of what talent they need. They are not certain about the precise skills profile, job specs take a long time to finalise and there is disagreement about timing, location and reporting lines. And this "disagreement" can drag on for a long time. For example, is a User Experience expert best reporting to Marketing or to IT, should e-Commerce candidates report into Operations or Marketing, should Heads of Data report into IT or Finance or Marketing or given their importance to driving future success perhaps direct into the CEO?

All these are legitimate questions and concerns but they can take months to resolve and often end up in unsatisfactory compromise. There is however an alternative. Instead of trying to decide these issues in theory, better to identify in practice. And for a number of leading companies now like Novartis, Adobe, Aviva, Barclays, Intel and others, the answer lies in using the recruiting process *"to meet and learn"*.

This means using the process very deliberately to meet a range of prospective candidates for a specific role. Let's say it's a Head of Digital. So the company will work with a recruiter to find such candidates from very clear but different targeted backgrounds. Some may have come up through the IT ranks, some through Marketing, some through Customer Operations and Experience. But the idea is: let's meet a sample of such candidates, let's arrange for the say 3 key internal stakeholders to meet that sample, and through that process, through meeting and interview, through questioning and getting to know different candidates, so let's use that to help us determine what the right sort of profile is and so crystalise what we do need, and what we don't, what is the right sort of background and profile that will work for us, our culture, our business needs and our organisation.

This recruitment process is set up with the clear recognition that it may indeed not lead to a final hire. But what it will do is provide the empirical, in-market insight and evidence and end the uncertainty and the continued internal and somewhat theoretical debate.

If it should lead to a hire then all the better. But an alternative and very satisfactory outcome can be to shortcut months of debate and uncertainty, align around the right candidate profile, clarify and confirm the focus and goals of the job spec and be able then to quickly go back to the market with a clear brief and clear knowledge of exactly what looking for. And that can lead to a quick and very rewarding hiring process for all.

This sort of recruitment process, to learn about the candidate market, and to resolve internal uncertainties, has been pioneered by the GAFA companies (Google, Amazon, Facebook and Apple). They will often use this approach and method as their Stage 1 recruiting process. They are very clear with the candidates from the outset as to what they are looking to achieve. And for candidates it can also be an attractive way to get to know an organisation, establish contact, get a foot in the door and if not this role, then be on the radar screen at the company in case something more suitable and relevant comes up in the future.

So it can be win:win and why not. With the talent war set to become even more intense then companies must use every opportunity to move ahead, cut out the delaying factors and be able to find and capture key talent at speed.

Chapter 13

5 keys to finding the best digital talent

Digital has now of course become part of every successful organisation's DNA. It has developed rapidly and offers new ways of working, quicker and more cost-effective solutions as well as providing new routes to customers and markets. It's become an engine of change as well as revenue growth and vanguard companies are experiencing substantial upsides in business.

At the same time, this catalyst for change is still a relatively new phenomenon and it means that the talent pool that has real depth of experience and expertise and know-how is relatively limited. Some companies are now saying that it is becoming very hard for them to find good "digital" talent; that they are struggling to support and develop the growth opportunities because they cannot get the right people into their teams.

But the most successful companies do not seem to find this same problem. Those companies who "get" digital, who fully embrace it from the CEO and HR to the most junior assistant, those for whom it has become their way of working and the source of growth as well as saving cost, those where there is real commitment, investment and priority behind their digital transformation programmes, those are the companies that have also learned how to build a really simple but very effective digital talent-finding and recruiting model. This chapter looks at those best practices.

One immediate observation is that these "best practices" are far from being rocket science. In many ways they are nothing new, they are no more than what good talent finding processes should anyway be all about. But in these days when the "digital talent pool" is still growing and when there is very high demand for the best people, then these "better processes" and practices become all the more compelling.

1. The Senior management team buys into the essence of Digital as their key driver.

How many times do candidates ask this…does the management team at senior level really get this, are they paying lip service to digital technology, to Cloud and web and e-commerce and mobile, or is this centre stage of their investment strategy? Good candidates say they repeatedly come across organisations who say they want to change, to embrace these new opportunities, but who in practice are doing very little that's different.

And candidates have wised up to this. It's one of their first questions. How important is this to the Board, how critical is this to the company's agenda, what levels of budget and support will be available? How often do candidates go to an interview and ask these leading questions, only to be disappointed and frustrated by the answer. They discover that in fact they will be in effect a "lone wolf", relegated to being a "voice of influence" (sometimes euphemistically described as a "champion of change"), that there will be no team to support them, that "this year there is very little budget, but next year…"

The best candidates will not be fooled. They will have been through these foundation experiences, they will have seen the pitfalls and frustrations. They will be looking for a place where they *can* make an impact and effect change.

Needless to say those organisations who want to do something but who don't back up the words with substantive commitments will not attract and get the best people.

2. Acknowledging that this need for digital-led change is now urgent and that all is not perfect!

Many companies are relatively weak in their digital know-how today, their IT legacy systems are poor and unsuited to new ways of working, their online environment is not optimised for the user experience and concepts of fundamental IT innovation are discussed but rarely pursued.

Yet in candidate interviews, it's as though there's a big cover-up. Instead of acknowledging the weaknesses or better put, "the opportunities for change", the interview is more about joining the team, fitting-in with existing work patterns, joining the culture, about gentle evolution when sometime more progressive and radical action is required.

But, the best digital talent is usually passionate about what can be done, big believers in what new technology solutions can achieve and wants to find an environment where they can practice what is preached. And be able to do so with immediate effect. As soon as they sense an organisation is slow or reluctant then once again they will themselves be very hesitant about joining such a culture.

3. A fast recruitment process

Good candidates respond positively and enthusiastically when the company also operates in that same way. From brief to first contact to final interview the process should take just a few weeks. It should not take months. And unfortunately months is the timeframe that many, often apparently very sophisticated large companies, will operate in. How many times does a business /function leader give out a brief, only for it then to stall while others sign-off, and then the key interviewer is busy or travelling or away, and then several weeks go by after the first interview before the second interview is set-up and then similar long gaps, and while for the candidate this process is potentially very much the centre of their whole world as they contemplate what for them is a big career move, this same sense of priority, of importance, of care and concern is often just not mirrored by the interviewing company.

Disillusion can quickly set in as the candidates starts to question: is this role really important to the company, are they committed to this new venture /initiative, they might be giving me good feedback but do they really want to make this hire, why do I have to wait weeks to hear if there is going to be a next step.

These delays should be the exception, but in practice they are common. Suffice to say that in this "war for good digital talent" those who interview quickly and positively get the best people (and see the earlier chapter on "Winning in the talent wars").

4. Some salary/ comp. flexibility

Because "digital" is new, because the talent pool is limited, because things are changing fast, then to maximise recruitment success, the learning is the need for at least some salary /comp. package flexibility.

Of course it's understood by candidates that the company will have salary bands at different levels in the company, that the compensation needs to approximately match up to peers, and that the new digital exec cannot be too much out of line.

But the fact is that there is a premium on salary levels for the best talent. That the best people will be paid well, that if it comes to making an offer, then the best out of this limited talent pool might just justify a premium to the base pay, or some kind of "sign-on" signature, or some higher grant of options or some inducement that does reflect their worth in the market.

It sometimes happens that a candidate will turn down job opportunities for roles they would be brilliant for simply because at the final negotiation the salary offered was below expectations or was less than that from a more progressive rival company.

Why is it that Google, Apple, Amazon and eBay are regarded as having the best digital talent today? One reason is that they did not compromise in paying the best salary levels to attract the top talent. Their mantra is: "the best companies should attract the best people". It might have been regarded as a significant investment in their early days to pay high compensation levels but they argue that that investment has more than paid back with their continued streams of market-leading innovations.

5. Measure how effective the recruitment process is /where it can be improved

There are certain key metrics which enable an organisation to measure how effective it is at finding and recruiting the best people:

- average time a job role is open
- ave. number of candidates interviewed per role
- ave. number of interviews a candidate has
- time from brief to offer
- % offers accepted
- ave. salary premium if any

- time from brief to candidate starting
- ave. length of time new hire stays with the company
- % who stay > 2 years

This dashboard /scorecard, combined with other metrics key to a specific organisation, can be kept and monitored. It may just highlight where things can be improved!

★★★★★

Finally, let's acknowledge that there are many brilliant people out there but they don't all need to be a rockstars to make a superb contribution

Recent work by a combined HR team from Caterpillar, General Mills and Schlumberger showed that a key delaying factor in recruitment was being too idealistic and setting unrealistic expectations of the profile and required abilities in the job description and brief.

The research showed that briefs often set out a "wish list" of desired attributes and expertise. And it concluded that often times no candidate could realistically be expected to match that wish list! It also showed that against those search criteria the level of salary offered often just would not be enough to attract that sort of person anyway.

So companies will frequently set off down a path where it will be very hard to find the right match. Hence there is delay and frustration with the process. The recommendation from the research is, put simply, be realistic!

There are many talented people out there who will do a very good, honest and often a tremendous job, but they are not all rockstars! They don't all walk on water! And do they need to, to do this particular job really well?

"Hire people with potential, give them the opportunity to spread their wings, put the right compensation behind them, watch them fly"

-Jack Welch, previous CEO of GE

"It's not about the coffee, it's about the people and growing and nurturing and teaching them so they can fulfil their potential"

-Howard Behar, founder of Starbucks

"Get the team together, only then can you make something happen"

-Thomas Watson, former President of IBM

Chapter 14

Technology impact on employee and talent management

The rapid advance of technology is impacting the HR function as much as any part of the business. Driven by AI and VR (virtual reality), technology solutions in the HR field are getting smarter and faster and HR professionals are finding they need to become increasingly tech-savvy, agile and innovative.

Some commentators ask if the HR function is ready to ride "the impending tsunami of change". But a Forbes survey encouragingly found that 69% of HR teams have been actively taking steps to embrace new tech tools and ideas and where appropriate roll out new solutions across the whole company.

Looking at Talent management particularly there appear to be 7 key changes:

1. AI chatbots

While AI can take many forms, there is a growing increase in the uptake of AI-enabled chatbots to screen and match candidates with jobs.

In a recent survey by Allegis, 58% of candidates were comfortable interacting with AI and recruitment chatbots in the early stages of the application process. An even larger percentage – 66% – were comfortable with AI and chatbots taking care of interview scheduling and preparation.

Today's candidates are aware the recruiting process might not be human-to-human at every touchpoint, but value the chance to receive information in whatever way they can. Randstad found 82% of job seekers believe the ideal recruiter interaction is a mix between innovative technology and personal, human interaction.

A recruitment chatbot can:

- collect information from candidates such as their CV/resume and contact information
- ask screening questions about candidates' experience, knowledge, and skills
- rank candidates on metrics such as qualifications, engagement, or recent activity
- answer FAQs about the job and the application process
- schedule an interview with a human recruiter

All of this information can be collected simultaneously from hundreds to thousands of candidates. This information can then be fed into the HR evaluation systems or sent directly to an individual recruiter to follow up on those the AI highlights.

Over time, the machine learning component of the chatbot will begin to understand which metrics it should be looking for based on the data it collects and rank candidates accordingly.

As this automation develops, so recruiters will be freed to spend more time adding value to the sourcing and selection process, conducting interviews and making offers to a considerably reduced and select pool of candidates. It could lead to a more streamlined and effective talent acquisition process and experience.

2. AI productivity

Technology automating HR practices has been around for a long time now, but the shift is now towards making the whole world of work easier. As a result systems that help people work more efficiently together, do more work in less time, or cope better with work-life balance are on the rise. More tech is likely to emerge that can drive better productivity and engagement across the whole organisation.

AI will be able to automate essential administrative processes (e.g. indexing and filing candidate records), onboarding, measuring performance and offering personalised curated learning content. In turn, HR professionals will be able to focus efforts on strategic workplace initiatives and contributing real business value.

Many common daily tasks will lend themselves to AI automation. That said, automation doesn't necessarily equate to the loss of human jobs. In fact, it may bode well for augmenting current HR roles by eliminating low productivity tasks and tapping into AI to make informed workforce decisions. The resulting improved efficiency and effectiveness of the HR function could be beneficial all round.

Josh Bersin, the enterprise learning /talent management leader comments that: "just as we see how many digital disruptors have toppled businesses in travel, retail, and other industries, we should essentially 'topple' our HR thinking with the adoption of digital solutions. HR organisations now have to learn how to 'be digital,' not just 'buy digital products."

As a brief example, Singapore-based OCBC Bank recently developed an in-house mobile app, HR In Your Pocket, giving employees a holistic HR resource center for submission of leave and claims, tracking medical and lifestyle benefits, and internal job postings. It also features an in-app chatbot to address questions employees might have about HR!

3. Employee mobility

The new currency of the labour market will be mobility, not stability. The balance of power in the employer/worker relationship is shifting in favour of the employee and research shows the growing numbers changing to freelance and contract modes of employment. As that happens, easy-to-use technology that is available 24/7 will be essential to help workers maintain connections across borders, managers lead their teams and drive collaboration.

Gartner estimates that by 2022, 60% of organisations will use a "unified talent management strategy" for their entire workforce – freelancers, contractors and employees – and this will encourage a more mixed workforce strategy, where eg contractors are seen as a core component of the team and not simply as a stop gap or interim solution to manage peaks of business or where the company is unable to find and recruit the longer term /perm hire.

4. Learning goes viral

The pressure is on for workers to constantly increase and update their skills. HR and businesses will play a crucial role in delivering learning that is continuous, consumable, relevant, and available on-demand. Traditional structured learning programmes will change to more self-directed social and informal learning platforms.

Small bursts of micro-learning will be reinforced through repetition in future lessons and tasks, as well as shared through social networking platforms. Moreover, social connectivity can encourage user-generated content and idea sharing, making learning more digestible and engaging. In place of fixed, formal content, this can lead to learning content spreading organically through an organisation with viral impact.

5. Insight into employees

Most companies are aware of the value inherent in employee feedback; between 50% and 75% of organizations administer workplace surveys to their employees. However, analysing and acting upon that data is another story. This data is rarely well analysed. A report from Luminoso showed that 52% of managers say that they review employee feedback but took no action on it, while 27% never reviewed the feedback at all.

Despite the challenge of processing and reviewing as many as hundreds of thousands of comments each time a survey is administered, the benefits of understanding employee feedback is clear. First and foremost, employee satisfaction and engagement has an impact on the bottom line. Organisations that enjoy a high level of employee engagement have on average 22% higher productivity than those who don't. In addition, employee engagement has a positive and measurable impact on retention. Organisations with highly-engaged employees report 25% to 65% less attrition than other companies, according to research from Gallup.

Advancements in AI and in natural language processing (NLP) have now dramatically changed the way employee insights can be analysed and implemented. They have made it possible for companies to collect, analyse, and respond to employee feedback on a monthly or biweekly basis, instead of quarterly or annually.

As an example, the HR analytics department at AT&T company wanted to better understand their employees' satisfaction levels. They had a clear understanding that higher employee satisfaction can lead to much better levels of customer service and have a significant impact on customer churn and retention. While the traditional statistical analyses they used worked well with quantitative data such as employee Net Promoter Scores, which measures employee engagement and motivation, they weren't as effective at processing unstructured, text-based data.

So previously, the HR team had resorted to pulling samples of employee and customer comments and reading through them manually. However, this was extremely time-consuming, and they feared that relying on people to comb through the data for insights exposed their analyses to bias – intentional or otherwise.

The team decided to switch to an AI- and NLP-based solution. They brought in a provider that could automatically pull in and aggregate employee and customer data from multiple sources. The provider's software relied upon AI, and as such could process the hundreds of thousands of comments within approximately five minutes – compared to the weeks it had previously taken the team to manually read through just a sample of the comments.

The time and resources that the team spent on processing data plummeted, enabling them to spend more time identifying the links between employee and customer concerns – especially identifying those who needed more training on products and systems. They also now had bandwidth to begin strategising how to address concerns and skill gaps, improve employee engagement and, through that, customer satisfaction.

6. Design thinking applied to HR

Traditional hierarchical organisation structures are being challenged. Replaced potentially by new organisational designs, such as the Spotify model described later, that better facilitate teamwork, agility and collaboration.

As more and more companies hire employees across different time zones, working on multiple projects and using various media, organisational design will need to evolve to accommodate a more fluid work stream. Fewer linear hierarchies, more matrix structures and employees may be measured increasingly on how they collaborate with internal and external networks.

This evolution in organisational design also warrants a shift in performance management. We can expect managers to be providing real-time feedback and coaching in place of fixed review cycles and that might in turn lead to investing in mobile performance coaching applications to facilitate and track performance discussions.

7. Augmented and virtual reality tools to amplify talent management

Virtual Reality (VR) will begin to find its way into the talent acquisition toolkits for HR recruiters. Candidates can expect to be served up interactive job advertisements, go on a VR tour of your future workplace in New York while sitting in Berlin, and complete VR assessments during your recruitment process. VR will also be used to enhance the employee experience by providing simulations of tasks and work challenges, better preparing workers for real-world situations before they have to face them.

As an example, Jet.com wanted to compete better with Amazon, and knew that will only happen if it pulls out all the stops and shows just how innovative it can be. The Walmart-owned online shopping platform is now leveraging its relaxed and collaborative company culture to attract top talent, utilising VR to create a "show, don't tell" experience. The initiative involves a full VR experience created by a design studio that allows prospective candidates to get a snapshot feel for the company's workspace and culture. From sitting in on a meeting with CEO, to enjoying the joys of Jet's happy hour and company band – along with some games, the immersive video simulates the experience of visiting Jet's US Hoboken office without the airfare.

Another example comes from the British Army. After offering VR experiences at events across the UK, the British Army saw its recruitment applications rise by 66%. Using a Samsung Gear VR headset, candidates could experience what it's like to engage in missions including driving a tank, parachuting, and mountaineering. They can also virtually experience the challenges of combat training.

★★★★★

Companies are learning that whether they immerse candidates in a full virtual world or not, the fact remains that to attract top talent, there is a growing need to up the candidate experience game.

Forbes has recently put together an HR Leadership Council and here are some of their recent key tips and ideas for securing the best candidates:

"Recruiting has gone Digital! Identify your target audience and how they behave in the digital world".

"Your organization's reputation permeates candidate decisions. What kind of presence does your organisation have online. Is it compelling?"

"Learn from Brand and Marketing colleagues to better position yourself in the market to have the greatest impact."

"Use social media. Organizations now have an opportunity to be visible to many. Candidates are doing their research prior to accepting interviews. They want to know what your current employees are saying about you. Take control of your company's image online!"

Chapter 15

Hub 'n Spoke

As Digital technology evolves at pace, many companies recognise the need to evolve their organisation and structure to adapt to the demands of the market place, to reflect the need to innovate, the imperative to deliver initiatives into the market quickly, the arrival of new technologies, new software tools, agile ways of working, Spotify type models (more on that in the next chapter) and the general need to be more customer engaging and responsive across multiple channels and touch points.

We only have to consider the continued and rapid penetration of e-commerce and online social media activity to realise just how critical it is to be able to respond to these market challenges, and opportunities!

e-Commerce is at c.25% and rising as a proportion of all retail sales in China. That figure is around 20% in the UK, one of the most highly developed and sophisticated multi-channel economies in the world, where spend per head online is higher than in any other country. Other Asian markets like Korea also see high levels of e-commerce activity and while in the US, as a %, e-commerce is at the c. 15% mark, it is in absolute $spend terms a substantial impact and affecting bricks n'mortar retailer survival.

The chart here below looks at the extraordinary and continued rise and growth of retail e-commerce and forecasts for the next few years:

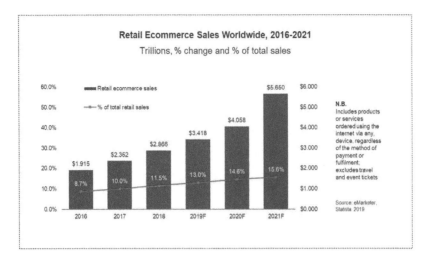

To respond to this multi /omni-channel challenge, companies are looking at a variety of different organisation models and solutions. And they are going through a journey which depends on their state of readiness and maturity and appetite for change.

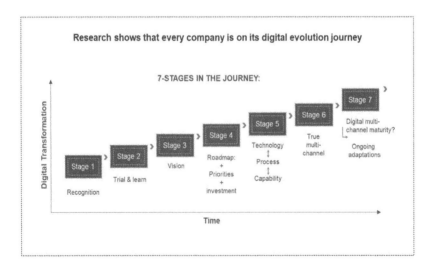

But MIT recent research has shown that despite often a keen recognition of the need for organisational change and development, that "only 7% of companies interviewed have successfully integrated new ways of working reflecting this new technology age…many are still mired in legacy systems, processes and ways of working and are still structured along traditional lines".

So what new multi-channel structure and organisation options should be considered?

One solution which is gaining much traction is the simple Hub n Spoke. It's not a new idea, which by itself makes it more intuitive and readily acceptable, and it does build on how many companies are already partly organised. But this now can become the fundamental matrix around which the whole organisation can be structured.

Essentially, this establishes a core Hub team at the centre. This is where core skills around Group and Customer Strategy reside, and where certain other defined capabilities should be. It's the centre of excellence which is setting the roadmap and blueprint for the future, and then governing, measuring, monitoring, intervening, fine-tuning the company's agenda and priorities.

The spokes can be in countries or in individual business units. This is where the core customer engagement sits, the heart of the sales and marketing, and the teams driving revenue growth.

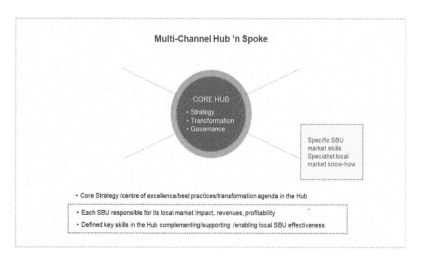

Hub n Spoke is an organisation model vigorously pursued by the likes of Dell, Cisco, Intel, HP and Experian. They are constantly adapting it to best fit their strategic needs and also the relative maturity and ability in each business unit and operating country. If the SBU is mature and of significant critical mass, then certain elements of the hub can be delegated. If that is not the case, then the Hub can exercise greater control and management. An example might be financial control, does the Hub do the management accounts of the SBU or can it now trust the SBU to do that and just have a final audit oversight. Another example might be around data and analytics, is the SBU of sufficient size that its P&L can afford and justify having its own D&A team, simply providing the streams of insights to the Hub by way of reporting. Or does the Hub retain that D&A "centre of excellence" so that it can much more firmly direct the SBU, set targets, monitor compliance and ensure delivery.

In the multi-channel context, the Hub can be responsible for overall Strategy, vision and targets. It might retain certain core skill areas which benefit from developed expertise and scale. That might be Production, Procurement, Media Buying and placement, key agency and partner relationships. Meantime, the spokes can focus on their local customers and consumers. They will be closer to them, often in terms of geography, but also in terms of day-to-day contact, proximity to local culture and customs, awareness of customer needs, ability to respond most quickly and effectively. They might therefore, and typically will, have the sales and marketing tools and responsibilities and to be most accountable for revenues and growth.

Arcadia, the UK retail group, is one example:

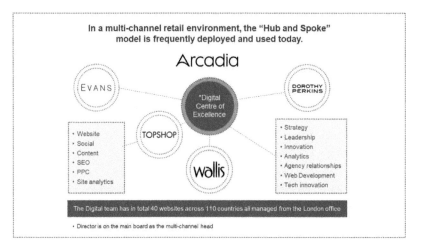

Another example is Unilever:

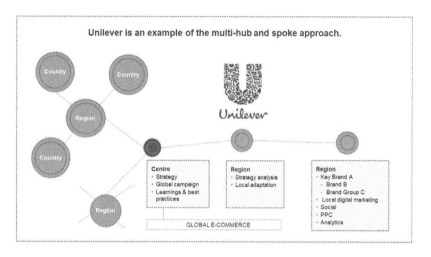

Determining what best sits in the Hub or in the Spoke can also be considered according to these 7 criteria which have been developed in empirical research carried out by Capgemini:

Hub n Spoke: 7 Guiding Principles

1. Hub in principle always responsible for Strategy, priorities, governance and financial control
2. SBU /Country in principle always responsible for local customer revenues and profit
3. Hub always champion, collector, disseminator (and enforcer) of best practices
4. Hub-based skills located there to also capture scale /centre of excellence advantages to reduce duplication and capture synergies
5. Hub Spoke balance with care, trading-off synergy while still empowering local SBU autonomy and entrepreneurialism
6. As the individual SBU develops, so the "Spoke" team and skills base can grow.
7. Constantly evolving and the balance between Hub and Spoke will vary by SBU *and* at stages in time.

There's no right or wrong organisation solution and simply copying what another has done can be counter-productive, especially if it does not fit the culture and style and state of the particular company and organisation. Hub n Spoke however is an inherently flexible framework, broad enough to potentially fit most any company while yet encouraging specific and better decision-making. The success of this structure, as with any other organisation solution depends on how well it is communicated and implemented. Do the employees understand the rationale behind any organisation change, do they "buy-in" and support it, does it seem like a natural next step for them, and so easy to transition to?

All these questions and others can be easily explored at the very early stages when such a structural solution is being considered. And some might be more ready for their "spoke" responsibilities than others! As summarised in a recent Bain & Company report: "Hub n Spoke can be an ideal solution to drive growth, empowering local employees to act as entrepreneurs and enabling the Hub to control costs and efficiency… we see this being deployed by many multi-nationals".

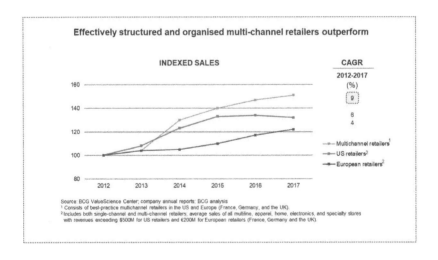

Chapter 16

Spotify – case study

Finding the Balance between Employee Autonomy and Accountability

Autonomy may be the single most important element for creating engagement in a company. How can anyone feel engaged, let alone inspired, if they feel that some supervisor is always looking over their shoulder? But autonomy is a double-edged sword. On the one hand, it spurs creativity and involvement. On the other, unchecked autonomy can lead to ambiguity and inefficiencies, even organisational chaos. To find the right balance, the research suggests two key challenges:

Balancing autonomy and accountability. A company has to establish a strategy and a purpose that provide context for employees' actions. It has to put the strategy into practice with measurable objectives, consistent measurement of progress toward those goals, feedback systems to monitor activities along the way, and appropriate consequences for reaching or failing to reach the goals. At their best, companies realise that not everything is easily measurable, or should be measured, and that constant temperature taking and micromanagement are inefficient and demoralising. So the better practice organisations prefer to establish boundaries and clear expectations, provide accountability but find the balance to allow autonomy. Where an effective balance is achieved, then employees and teams know they will be held accountable, and yet they also know where the guardrails are. They understand the objectives, and they can have a great deal of freedom in determining how to reach them within those guardrails. Clarity of purpose and what are high-resolution strategies, which give people a clear view of where they're headed, can provide the compass that can guide the choices that teams and individuals make.

Balancing freedom to innovate versus following proven routines. The art and science here is determining how to get both outcomes — consistency and innovation — in the right proportion and in the appropriate parts of your organisation. In many areas, freedom to innovate is the critical need. Think of new product development, or the parts of the company's value chain and business model that are undergoing significant reinvention because of digital transformations. In these activities, speed of innovation is critical, and the rallying cry should be autonomy, small teams, and organisational agility. Other areas, however, may benefit from standardised approaches. These are areas where consistent outcomes are essential and where speed of execution comes from deploying common methods, best practices, and enforced routines. The focus here should be on repeatability and efficiency. Each requires speed in different areas, innovation versus execution, and achieves these results in different ways.

The challenge in striking the right balance is to know which method should predominate and how to design appropriate ways of working for each area.

A favourite example now often quoted and illustrating how to potentially approach these challenges is the Swedish company Spotify. Spotify was founded in 2006, and now a leading music, video, and podcast streaming company with close to 100 million paying subscribers and $5 billion in revenue.

Its more than 3,500 employees are organized into agile teams, called squads, which are self-organizing, cross-functional, and co-located. Spotify has largely succeeded in maintaining an agile mindset and principles without sacrificing accountability. It enables innovation while keeping the benefits of repeatability, and it creates alignment without excessive control. Some of its lessons can potentially apply to many companies, not just digitally enabled service providers.

Spotify's core organizational unit is an autonomous squad of no more than eight people. Each squad is accountable for a discrete aspect of the product, which it owns cradle to grave. Squads have the authority to decide what to build, how to build it, and with whom to work to make the product interoperable. They are organised into a light matrix called a tribe. Tribes comprise several squads linked together through a chapter, which is a horizontal grouping that helps to support specific competencies such as quality assistance, agile coaching, and web development. The chapter's primary role is to facilitate learning and competency development throughout the squads.

Leadership within the squad is self-determined, while the chapter leader is a formal manager who focuses on coaching and mentoring. Spotify believes in the player-coach model: Chapter leaders are also squad members. Squad members can switch squads and retain the same formal leader within their chapter. Spotify introduced another organisational element, known as a guild. Guilds are lightweight communities of interest whose primary purpose is to share knowledge in areas that cut across chapters and squads, such as leadership, continuous development, and web delivery.

This unusual combination of squads, tribes, chapters, and guilds is the organisational infrastructure that underlies Spotify's operating model. At first reading, it might sound like just another way to define a conventional organisational matrix in Millennial- and digital-friendly terms. But a closer examination reveals just how different the model really is and why it seems to work so well.

The squad structure works in teams no bigger than 12 and even as Spotify has grown it helps the company still feel small and manageable. The squads are fully autonomous and 100% responsible for a single feature. In a way it's seen as having lots of small start-ups (squads) that harness the power of the bigger company by combining expertise (guilds and chapters) while creating alignment through tribes and alliances.

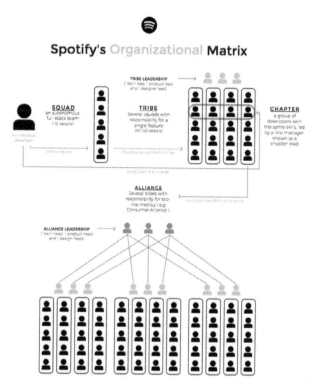

Spotify's Organizational Matrix

The squad structure achieves autonomy without sacrificing accountability. Every squad owns its features throughout the product's life cycle, and the squads have full visibility into their features' successes and failures. There is no single appointed leader of a squad; any such leadership role is emergent and informal. Results are visible both through internal reviews and through customer feedback, and squads are expected to fully understand successes and failures. Squads go through end of term analyses of failures to ensure learning, and some squad rooms have "fail walls." Every few weeks, squads conduct retrospectives to evaluate what is going well and what needs to improve.

To ensure that the feedback process is effective for individuals as well as for the squads, Spotify redesigned its performance management system to separate salary discussion and performance evaluations from coaching and feedback. Before, peer feedback was incorporated into salary reviews; in Spotify's words, that "incentivised people to gather as many favourable reviews as possible rather than getting feedback around their biggest areas of potential improvement." Now, colleagues use an internal tool to invite anyone — including managers, peers, and direct reports — to provide feedback on results and on what an individual can do to improve. Employees may solicit feedback as often as they choose..."the result is a process that everyone needs to own and drive themselves — it is about development and personal growth."

- **Continuous improvement:** both personally, and in the wider organisation.
- **Iterative development:** short learning cycles to validate assumptions as quickly as possible.
- **Simplicity:** Simplicity is the mantra guidance during scaling for methods of working and organising the organisation.
- **Trust:** "we trust our people and teams to make informed decisions about the way they work and what they work on."
- **Servant leadership:** a focus on coaching, mentorship, and solving problems rather than telling people what to do.

Culture plays a big role in keeping the innovation engine firing on all cylinders. Spotify has an experiment-friendly culture with an emphasis on test-and-learn approaches and contained experiments. If people don't know the best way to do something, they are likely to try alternative approaches and run several A/B tests to determine which is preferable. In place of opinion, ego, and authority, Spotify say they work hard to substitute data, experimentation, and open dialogue about root causes.

Spotify fosters alignment without excessive control. The central organisational feature that shapes Spotify's model is the concept of "loosely coupled, tightly aligned squads." The key belief here is that "alignment enables autonomy — the greater the alignment, the more autonomy you can grant." That's why the company spends so much time aligning on objectives and goals before launching into work. The leadership model at Spotify reinforces this alignment. A leader's job is to figure out the right problem and communicate it, so that squads can collaborate to find the best solution. Coordination comes through context and through a deep understanding of the company's priorities, product strategies, and overall mission. The ability to release features and then flex them enables full releases even before all features are fully operational. Here, too, the culture acts as a support. The watchword at Spotify is "be autonomous, but don't suboptimise — be a good citizen in the Spotify ecosystem." A common analogy at the company is a jazz band: Each squad plays its instrument, but each also listens to the others and focuses on the overall piece to make great music.

Clearly, not all of Spotify's choices will be appropriate for every company. But the Spotify approach is a benchmark which seems to work very well for them and an exemplar as to how companies can change the way they organise to be able to move at pace and impact in this digital world. Companies need to make explicit choices in their operating model, ways of working, and culture that can address core tensions between individual autonomy and organisational goals. The goal is to get alignment without excessive control and at heart build an engaging and inspiring working environment.

A number of companies are now actively looking at this Spotify organisation model and wondering if this might be the next stage of their own evolution. They admire the Spotify culture of innovation and fast pace market development, they can see how that has helped the company grow fast and drive to a global market leadership, they see that people in the company appear genuinely committed to it and to its future success. They care. So companies wonder, can we implement the same sort of model?

But when companies do copy the 'Spotify model', it can sometimes happen through a top-down directive, without perhaps taking a close enough look at what kind of culture and leadership is needed to make it work.

Often the existing structure is simply changed, overnight, into a new matrix blueprint, an organisation model that is suddenly labelled with Squads, Chapters, and Tribes and with some expectation and notion that this will transform the company into a fast-paced high-growth innovative and dynamic organisation which will barnstorm to market leadership. Instead of, perhaps, looking at culture and ways of working and growing an evolutionary structure that's right for a particular organisation and is able to take-on a change agenda.

Implementing a Spotify solution, as some large established corporations seem to be doing, can just create confusion and complexity. It might be right for a 50-person start-up, but for a 5000-person+ multi-national corporation with legacy systems and processes, it could be a high cost and high risk move.

Just as startups like Spotify focused the right organisation culture and model *for them,* so every organisation needs to find its own "organisation-fit". That might involve adopting some elements of this Spotify solution, or even all of it, but only after careful check and examination.

"Stop trying to borrow wisdom and think for yourself. Face your difficulties and think and think and think and solve your problems yourself. Suffering and difficulties provide opportunities to become better. Organisation success is through hard work and never giving up."

-from Taiichi Ohno, a leading Japanese guru on organisation structure

Chapter 17

Building the Digital team

Why are some companies being especially successful in this digital world? How did children's wear retailer Zulily.com grow from zero to more than $1bn in revenues in less than 5 years, Kraft's Nabisco launch a new product line which achieved $100m of sales in 1 year, RELX Group migrate from being a print publisher to a highly regarded digital information software business, Barclays Bank forge ahead of its rivals as a "digital first" innovator, Amazon achieve its extraordinary market sector penetration and customer engagement? What are these types of companies doing to exploit the new, still fast-changing digital landscape and achieve that winning market position?

The answer lies in how they organise for digital, how they build their teams and their skills sets, how they develop a culture inside that is supportive and encouraging of digital innovation and development, how they share and learn, how they attract and retain key talent who can make the difference. They've got Digital into their mainstream, into their DNA, they realise its importance but most critically they act and behave and implement and deliver and reward for digital initiative and success.

There are 6 key decisions that need to get made if a company is to join these digital winners. These are around:

1. *Structure and Organisation*
2. *Leadership and Engine room*
3. *Skills and Scale*
4. *Culture and Style*
5. *Learning and Sharing*
6. *Talent Finding and Retaining*

Let's look at each in turn. Before we do it's worth reminding of the Facebook mantra that is written large on the walls of their office: "The journey is just 1% finished". Facebook recognise and appreciate that "we've only just begun in our ambitions and what can be achieved". And it is a journey, not just for Facebook, but for all companies. The technology landscape continues to change at breath-taking speed, it's hard for any individual or company to keep up, the boundaries of what's possible and what is not keep changing, the potential for disruption in the market is never-ending, new possibilities and potential in existing and in new markets are surfacing all the time. This "technology revolution" that we are living through is still in its early stages. And just as the market place keeps evolving, so the journey for companies stretches out into time as an organisation tries to assimilate and absorb and process what all these changes may mean for its future, for what to invest in, what to prioritise, what skills and organisation shape and what technology changes required to capture these market opportunities and deliver continued shareholder value.

Many companies struggle with all the change opportunities, want to leapfrog and jump to some higher technical plane, but while that ambition may be laudable, it needs to come with the recognition that it does all take time. Leapfrogging for an established corporation is hard to do, in fact it's difficult for any company to make successful changes and even step-changes in the way it operates. So what's critical is, yes have the ambition for sure, have the clear goals and sense of mission and purpose. But put that into the context of what can the organisation cope with, how ready is it for change, what external catalysts and support and hiring is required to enable and facilitate these changes, what's the right timeframe and timetable that allows for the current business operations to keep going and developing even while new ways of working and new levels of customer engagement take shape and can begin to make their impact.

1. Structure and Organisation

A common question is: should we keep Digital as a separate stand-alone team and group or should we simply have it all somehow integrated into the core of the company?

Digital started off in every organisation as a separate group and team. There were these specialist skills such as Search engine optimisation, SEO and SEM, and such people were often pioneers, evangelists, sometimes technical geeks who did things and seemed to know things that others in the company barely understood but had been convinced were nevertheless somehow important for their customers. And of course, that "specialist" digital unit started to grow adding other skills such as "front end web developers", content writers, web designers, email marketers, web analysts… Over a short space of time a few specialists, at least in the larger organisations became a large team. And what's more, instead of just managing a bit of online brochureware, they were starting to drive ever larger chunks of revenue. Suddenly this team became the growth engine of the company.

At retailer John Lewis for example, so specialist and important did this team become, that they had their own offices in a separate building with its own team managers, culture, ways of working and doing its own thing, a mystery and black box to the rest of the organisation, more than 150 people, somehow though justifying themselves as they drew more and more plaudits from commentators and customers and became responsible for a sizeable percentage of the JL business.

For JL, there came a point where this mystery had gone on too long. There was a felt need to learn, to absorb, to transfer this customer and market know-how and get the whole organisation on-board with this way of thinking and engaging with customers. So the separate office was shut, the digital team was brought back into the head office, front end developers were reconnected with the IT team, online marketers were made a part of the wider company Marketing team, people were integrated. But still not completely. There is still a Head of Online and Digital who manages eg the specialist online marketers. That Head of Online may report to the equivalent of the CMO, but the digital team have still kept their distinctiveness and the organisation is forced to acknowledge that however much it may desire complete integration, that that goal today is just not possible, that there is need for specialists with particular skills and expertise. Yes make sure what they do is part of the overall long term customer vision and plan, but accept too that they need to move and innovate and operate often in a distinctive style and way and need to be given the scope to test and trial new market place ideas all the time.

This John Lewis vignette is mirrored in many other companies today. Should we leave the specialists to get on with it, or, if we "bring them back in", then will we lose that expertise and dilute the market potential? On the other hand, doesn't the whole organisation need to be working to an integrated multi-channel agenda? Shouldn't everyone be somehow involved now in this tech-led world?

To answer this question, it's critical to acknowledge and respect that each and every organisation is different. Every company is at different stages of its digital journey. If Facebook feel they are only at 1% then where are the long established corporations? Are the likes of eg Shell or Philips or Procter & Gamble still only at the starting gate? Or has each in its own way in fact been effectively laying the foundations and building the capabilities that will enable it to succeed in a digital world? Each company has different culture, style and ways of thinking, each is at its own state of digital maturity and readiness and that as much as anything will determine and define how it organises and how it evolves, what it keeps specialist and what it integrates. But for most every company, the vision of a fully integrated, "we are all now digital" environment and organisation structure is still a long way off.

To help understand how any one particular organisation should structure its digital teams, the following sections can add perspective on how others are doing it and what needs to be considered in making the decision.

2. Leadership and Engine room

Who should lead the Digital charge? It's now become so critical to so many companies' futures, that it has become a c-suite role. We now see an ever-growing number of "Chief Digital Officers" being appointed. This can reflect the growing recognition of just how much of the company's business is now dependent on being successful in this space.

This "elevation" of digital to the senior ranks has at the same time brought a number of tensions, especially in the relationship of the CDO with the CMO and CIO (too many "c's"?).

For example, who is responsible for the customer? Historically that responsibility would naturally have been the remit of the CMO. But if there is a CDO and eg half the revenues are online, then shouldn't perhaps the CDO have equal responsibility? And if so how does that "responsibility" get shared, who makes the final call?

This can get even more complicated where online becomes the majority of the business. If the CDO has P&L responsibility and is acknowledged as being the leader of that, then why is there a need for a separate group CEO, shouldn't the CDO in effect become the CEO?

All this is just a further illustration of the still relative immaturity of digital, or put another way, it's an example of where most companies are on their journey that this sort of issue is only just beginning to surface and has not yet been answered or addressed.

While this leadership battle rages away, there is also a next level challenge in the engine room. That is how best to organise and structure the digital teams, the key junior execs and mid-level managers who are building and driving and nurturing the business day by day. Part of this question is also where best to locate them. Is it a John Lewis type solution, should they remain separate, should they be integrated and if integrated then just how much!

One way of resolving this is to look at 3 companies by way of example, who have each adopted a similar structure. The 3 are Amazon.com, Costa Coffee and Next, the clothing retail group.

Each of these vanguard companies has realised how important it is to get its web sites and online presence optimised. They have realised that this is not a once-a-year review, but needs to be something continuous and ongoing, ideally 24/7 and if possible in real time.

Each has responded to this challenge by restructuring and reorganising 3 specific teams. That is (i) the front end web developers, (ii) the web analytics and insight group and (iii) the online marketing team. The decision was made that these 3 groups be brought together, be co-located and sat next to each other and also report into the same person. Usually that's the Marketing Director or could be the Head of Site Optimisation or in other companies even the Chief Customer Officer.

The web analytics team are constantly monitoring user journeys, fall out rates, which promotional offers are working and which are not, should a promotion be ended now, should the price be reduced or raised, should a call to action be made more prominent, put in a different colour, put in a different place on the web site, what's being said about the company, the products on social media, is any response needed, what else is happening externally with the weather, politics, sport, internationally that might influence or change what might work today, this hour, this minute online that could optimise the customer experience and maximise sales.

The web analytics team are identifying these change opportunities in real time, they share that with the Marketing /Commercial team who are charged with making immediate decisions on what to change if anything in response to the observed insights.

The front end web dev team then take over and make the changes, fast.

All this delivers a highly responsive, targeted, customised, digital operations environment that is looking at all that's going on, on desktop and mobile, and fine-tuning with agility and speed.

It is that type of "engine room" management and structuring that can make a tremendous difference to a company's success.

3. Skills and Scale

A significant challenge is how to afford the wide variety of specialists required to deliver the Digital potential. There seem to be any number of very distinct skill sets ranging through the value chain from Customer Awareness development through Customer Engagement and Conversion and then keeping them coming back!

The skills need necessarily to include some or all of SEO, SEM, online media display, affiliates, content, social media, creative design, conversion, analytics, e-commerce /transaction management, CRM, fulfilment, returns, technical web development, project management, mobile, partnerships and intermediaries, product /service strategy, roadmap and innovation…

Some companies just don't have the size and scale of budgets to afford to bring in specialists for each one of these areas. Many other companies do have the scale and budget potential but have other priorities or just don't appreciate and realise the need and value potential or have other pressures on costs and people.

The typical compromise is to bring in a few and ask them to multi-task, to work across the whole digital value chain and do their best to optimise where possible. Such an approach may be a fiscal necessity but it's important that an organisation does appreciate what skills it does *not* have and so adjusts its targets and expectations accordingly.

For some others, the solution involves bringing in contractors and freelancers for a particular project only and justifying that resource on the back of a specific project RoI. That can work well though clearly individuals hired on that temporary basis will sometimes lack the emotional engagement with the product and brand and the genuine desire and passion to go the extra mile to make this succeed.

An alternative solution is to set up a network of support agencies and consultancies who can advise and take on specific projects eg rebuild the web site.

Whatever the solution path that is chosen, it should be part of a long term strategy that looks at the role digital can play in an organisation and looks at a gradual build up in budgets and people and capabilities. Taking a purely year by year approach that is at best incremental and perhaps squeezes a 5% increase in spend and activity is unlikely to match the pace of change in the company's market place and the readiness of customers to embrace any digital initiatives the company does make.

B2B companies have been especially "guilty" of this slow incremental approach, looking at the slow pace of their competitors and using that to justify their own inactivity. But many such organisations have found that if they do invest and create an effective digital marketplace for their customers then it can have a significant impact and gets a surprisingly quick and positive customer response. Companies like Cisco, Intel, BP, Coats plc, BT, Pitney Bowes have all discovered that if they do divert resources and spend to Digital then *it does pay back.*

4. Culture and Style

Successful digital-led companies have developed 3 core elements to their culture:

- fostering an entrepreneurial spirit
- creating an agile environment of "test, trial and learn"
- recognising that we are going through an era of fast change and that there will be ambiguity and uncertainty and that that is ok!

The best digital people are often pioneers, they thrive on change, they look for adventure and the chance to explore possibilities, they aren't comfortable working in an environment where everything is set, where there's little room for manoeuver, they want to work fast and get things done, and not wait 6 months for IT to change some copy on the web site. They are more instinctively entrepreneurs, they thrive where that spirit is fostered and supported, they are comfortable with change and actually are prepared to push for that, ambiguity does not unsettle or discomfort them, on the contrary that is what they expect and what enables them to think and act and come up with disruptive solutions that can be game-changers.

In today's world, a winning business needs these sort of people in its midst. Such individuals can also help shift the whole corporate culture to a more focussed 21st century business model.

5. Learning and Sharing

Hyper Island is one of the world's leading learning and training centres for Digital. Its 3 day "Digital Masterclass" is almost legendary in its ability to convert doubting or uncertain execs into overnight digital evangelists. It's set up for groups of senior execs but can also be used at all levels across the company. There are usually around 30 in the class group and it's a full 3 day immersion, staying overnight, working hard in both lectures and workshops and presentations that share what others are achieving and driving out what could be possible.

Less a "class" than an introduction to a new way of thinking, it's intended as an intensive immersion and learning and there are other groups that do this as well including the major business schools like MIT, Columbia and INSEAD but the Hyper Island can appeal as it's more "short sharp e-shock".

There are also any number of seminars and conferences that seek to train and share best practices and latest ideas eg at the IDM (Institute of Direct Marketing) and at CIM (Chartered Institute of Marketing). For those who want to dig deeper there are longer training programmes such as the MSc (a part time /evenings /remote learning programme) in Internet Retailing at Manchester Metropolitan University and coordinated by e-Consultancy.

These courses do not just appeal to those who wish to learn. They also have a pivotal role where a group of execs in a company are trying to drive through digital change and technology innovation and encountering resistance and hesitation from colleagues whose support they need. If such colleagues can be persuaded to participate in some external education and enlightenment, then it can of course change the pace and direction of the company's development and investment.

This need for immersion, learning and training, for sharing ideas and expertise is all the more critical in the digital world. Things are moving fast, they are changing, new more agile start-up ventures are springing up out of nowhere challenging incumbents and disrupting decades long and traditional ways of thinking and operating. Innovations may be customer-facing but they can also be internal process-driven enabling eg lower costs of production or automating processes which can speed up time to market. It's near impossible to do the day job and stay up-to-date on all the potential disruptive forces at work, so sharing, training, listening to experts, finding, somehow, that occasional time to listen and learn, creating the environment at work which both encourages and enables that, that can all lay the foundations for a successful future.

6. Talent Finding and Retaining

Many say that they find it very difficult to attract key digital talent. They may find it takes months, perhaps even 6 to 9 months to find someone. In some cases, companies give up on that targeted hire altogether. They either make do, or have to reach out to some agency or consultancy to provide the resource and support.

Yet some companies have it seems no problem at all in quickly attracting the right sort of candidate profile. Whether it's a start-up like Zulily.com, a complex audit /advisory group like Deloitte, a B2B publisher like Incisive, manufacturer distributors like Huawei, Smith & Nephew and Brady or the likes of Tesco and Argos.

How do companies develop that talent attraction? The 7 simple keys are:

(i) A good quality online presence so that when the candidate looks up the company for the first time they get a good impression,

(ii) A good "digital story", a good explanation available as to where the company is on its digital journey, a recognition that there is a long way still to go, a sense of that adventure and what the goals are,

(iii) A commitment to digital from the CEO and through-out the corporation,

(iv) A readiness to invest, even modestly, in new ideas

(v) A fast-paced interview process that takes weeks not months

(vi) A reasonable amount of flexibility around the job spec so as not to exclude good, bright, fast-learning people who may not be able to tick all the boxes yet on the spec.

(vii) Flexibility, within reason, on pay and benefits.

Sometimes it may just eg need a small sign-on to compensate an exec for loss of bonus accrued at previous employ or need to buy a season ticket for the longer commute.

It just requires a readiness and desire to move quickly, be flexible and make it easy for the right candidates to say yes!

Another way of thinking about this is to reflect on the prospective employee "user journey". There's lots of talk and effort going into to the optimisation of the customer journey to maximise conversion. Much less attention has been paid to the *employee* experience and how that can be optimised to streamline hiring and make acceptance easy.

From the first contact to the last and then through to the on-boarding process, who in the company is responsible? HR initiate and coordinate but they require the hiring managers to do their bit and make time available, not cancel interviews at the last minute, give immediate feedback, be prepared properly for the interviews, recognise that for the candidate this can be a life-changing moment and so treat that moment with the respect it deserves.

Too often, even for relatively junior roles, there can be 6 to 12 interviews (in one case I know of 24!). It is of course almost impossible that a candidate will be liked by everyone they see. Does one "no" outweigh 9 "yes's"? That can often be the case. And as each interview is set up, so the timetable is drawn out, the weeks turn into months and meantime a faster-moving company comes in and snaps up the prospective hire.

Getting this right helps get the right candidate on board. But then they also need to be retained. Good digital people are on every recruiter's radar screen. They may just have moved jobs but they're still getting calls about new opportunities. So if the new job does not live up to expectations they can be seduced and intrigued by something elsewhere, "the grass is greener?"

★★★★★

By way of a summary, we can review the following Barclays case study, looking at how the Bank has become more "digital first".

From CEO Ashok Vaswani came a stream of communications about digital. His mantra: "Digitization is redefining and transforming our business".

This has included a wide number of initiatives. The target has been to educate the workforce and turn each and every employee into a digital evangelist. And through that galvanise and engage customers in a more digital-designed way. Vaswani's goal was for employees to become more digitally literate, to bring about new ways to connect with customers, to identify new business and revenue streams and to take advantage of new technologies.

Internally, people were encouraged to dress more comfortably, the work space was changed to include pods and chill-out areas, football tables appeared!, ties disappeared, seminars were held with the idea of teaching everyone about why digital is important and what that would mean.

Employees were encouraged to become "digital natives" and to participate in various training programmes inside the bank and externally too. "Reverse mentors" were set up, throughout the bank, so that senior execs were deliberately exposed to latest digital ideas and diplomatically encouraged to change ways of operating. The Bank launched its high profile Digital Eagles consumer publicity campaign ensuring that each and every branch had its own digital champion who could encourage consumers to use the newly installed self-serve machines rather than stand in line and wait for counter service. 12000 Digital Eagles have so far been trained to evangelise at branch level. Alongside this, is the Barclays Digital Code Playground, a widely-advertised initiative to encourage people to come to "learn to code" training sessions run for free in the Bank's local branches.

What does all this mean? It starts to change a whole culture across a huge and sprawling organisation. The employees feel the need to be a part of this as it starts to become an accelerated route for promotion and higher bonus levels. It also showcases the Bank in a different light, encourages renewed customer engagement and begins to change their perception of what Barclays can do for them.

Banks are unlikely to ever have a warm cuddly brand image, but they can move with the times, they can change what they stand for, they can use digital to streamline how they organise and operate, they can look for new ways of working that will make it easy for customers to use their services online and by mobile, they can create an environment where employees feel there is opportunity and adventure and that things are moving forward, they can help make themselves seen as the leading employer for digital servcies in the financial services sector, they can look to be a 2025 winner and leave other rivals behind.

Chapter 18

How to structure and organise the digital team?

Introducing the Digital /Multi-Channel Value Chain.

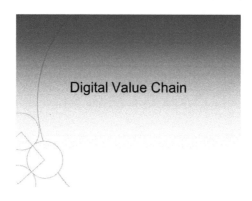

Digital Value Chain

Recent research from McKinsey shows a key agenda item is all around: *how should companies best organise to capture the increasingly critical digital opportunity?*

Some 63% in a recent survey said that they were unsure how to structure and fit digital skills into their existing teams. 31% felt that digital was now requiring a totally new look at skills, teams, reporting lines and ways of working. 27% also commented that "integrating new digital talent" was proving "surprisingly difficult!"

So what's causing this challenge and uncertainty? No-one doubts the importance of digital. Most every company, whether B2C or B2B, has seen how customers are demanding an increasingly online, automated, self-serve environment, how the customer expectation has rapidly developed for a seamless, integrated multi-channel experience, how getting that customer experience right can genuinely add incremental revenue and growth. So the need for people with digital skills and talent to drive this is clear. Whether in SEO or SEM, or effective e-mail marketing, or in user experience and site conversion, or in customer retention and CRM /database management, in site analytics or social media, whether via mobile or desktop…all these areas are acknowledged skills and areas of expertise which most every company nowadays recognises it needs to have.

The challenge seems to lie in the sheer size and range of new skills that a company must now embrace. Should we hire in all these different skills or can we focus on just a few, how can we budget for all this, can we see a way to get a return on this investment, how add these skills to the organisation while not upsetting the existing and still successful traditional routes to market and the people, experience and capabilities that go with that?

All the current advice on this seems to stay at the macro /30,000 feet level. It tries to answer questions like should there be a Chief Digital Officer, should digital report to the CMO or the CTO, should digital stand alone as a separate function or should it be integrated into one total group? But there's little or no advice below those big questions. They are still important but once they've been decided then how organise the next level down? How structure the junior and mid-level managers and their teams? Where do they fit in?

This chapter sets out a possible solution for this. It looks below the Director level, below the CMO or the CTO or the CDO! It takes a view as to how to organise the key skills at the coalface, the experts who are doing the detailed digital and multi-channel campaign, customer and business development.

To help with this we can identify a series of key principles and guiding criteria:

(i) *Set up the structure with no more than 6 direct reports to the c-Level exec in charge.*
(ii) *Keep it simple and manageable*
(iii) *Make it measurable!*
(iv) *Set things up in a multi-channel way so that that digital is integrated and not separated.*
(v) *Establish the team so that together they can take one holistic and seamless view of their customer.*
(vi) *Identify the key metrics and targets that can drive to a clear RoI on the persons or teams hired*
(vii) *Keep it flexible: digital is evolving fast and areas like content, social media, mobile and self-serve are becoming increasingly key drivers of success. They may at some point deserve and require more prominence in the team structure.*

Recent studies from WPP's Millward Brown, from e-Consultancy and also D-360's own on-the-ground experience show that this desired digital and multi-channel skills set can best be categorised or structured into 6 key skill areas. We can describe those categories as forming the *"multi-channel value chain"*.

The 6 key areas are:

- **Strategy** (that includes Brand and Product strategy and road-mapping)
- **Brand Awareness**
- **Consideration** (eg the content, social media, collateral that the prospective purchaser considers)
- **Lead Generation** (getting people onto the web site or eg into the call centre)
- **Conversion** (getting the sale)
- **Retention** (getting the customer to come back /make the next purchase, the "customer lifetime value").

We can map this out in this way.

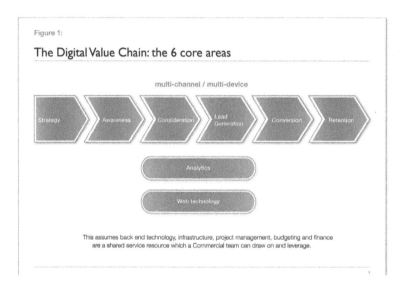

Figure 1:

The Digital Value Chain: the 6 core areas

multi-channel / multi-device

Strategy · Awareness · Consideration · Lead Generation · Conversion · Retention

Analytics

Web technology

This assumes back end technology, infrastructure, project management, budgeting and finance are a shared service resource which a Commercial team can draw on and leverage.

What we are looking at here is in effect the 6 key "Heads of Department" who would report into the c-Level Exec. They may each be directors in their own right. Or they may be "heads of" depending on size and type of company, resources and budgets and ultimately the level of ambition that the total company has. It's all about getting digital /multi-channel working at its most powerful and deliver its greatest potential.

So what's in each of these 6 departments or teams and why distinguish these 6 particular categories and stages in the value chain?

We can list out (Figure.2) the key areas of skill, remit, task and responsibility that each of these team heads can be expected to cover. The chart /table here is not intended to be exhaustive and it's certainly not a job profile. But it is a high level view of what can be expected and what's involved.

And this listing helps reinforce why these 6 distinct team areas have been defined and identified. It is because each area is specialist in its own right. Each does require particular and specific skills and expertise. Someone for example who is expert on UX may not also be expert at Product Strategy development. Equally, someone who is engaged in social media and content development will not necessarily be the best skilled person to eg drive database insight and CRM programmes. The skills are different. And to get the best from the team then the most efficient way to organise is to recognise that difference and structure accordingly.

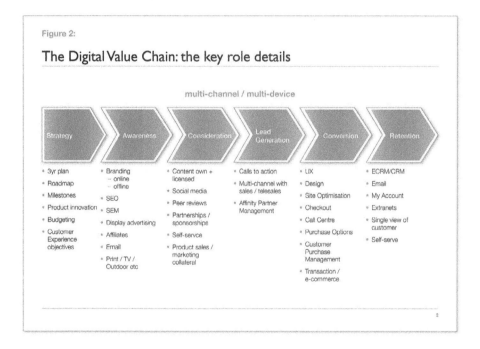

In early digital /multi-channel times, there was not the insight, the budgets, the returns available to start building out big teams with this sort of definition and distinction. Companies hired eg a "digital manager" and asked them to kind of oversee, well everything. Do the Search, the emails, the online advertising, the customer development, the e-commerce, the mobile app development etc. It is only in very recent times, that the scale and size of the multi-channel opportunity has grown such that this level and size of team does become possible and the RoI can be seen and quantified.

There is no question that it is a virtuous circle. Set up the team correctly, make that commitment and investment, set key goals and measures of success, target a clear RoI and drive toward that.

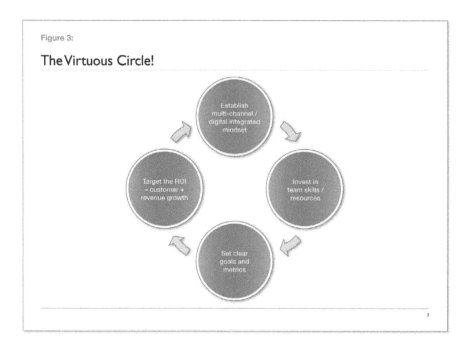

Figure 3:

The Virtuous Circle!

Figure. 4 below now shows the metrics of success, the drivers of that RoI and customer /revenue growth. It immediately shows again how very different each role is. It demonstrates clearly that a company needs its team defined and set up carefully so that there are expert people, with the right skills, able and empowered to focus on a specific set of goals.

Setting things up along these lines makes the job of the c-Level exec in charge of all this all the more manageable and achievable. That person now has 6 key reports. Each is responsible for a core and specific part of the customer multi-channel value chain. Each is tasked with a clear set of deliverables and metrics. A KPI dashboard can be set up incorporating the key metrics from each team at each stage of the chain. Success is all about getting all 6 teams to report continuing growth in their key metrics and ratios. Each is both a cost centre as well as a profit centre. If they are contributing in the right way, then their team is delivering. They can put forward investment proposals in their area and identify their potential RoI. That might be more resource or more funds or a new product /feature/service launch. But each step is therefore measurable and all the more manageable for it.

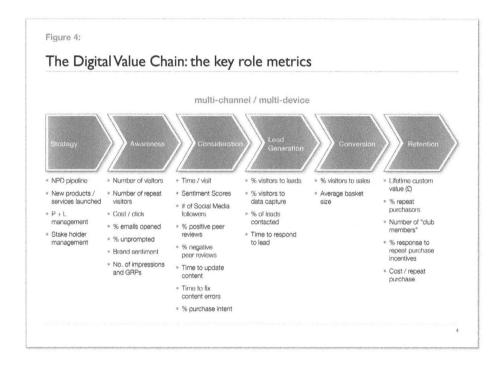

Figure 4:

The Digital Value Chain: the key role metrics

★★★★★

Any organisation research will always make the same observation: what is right for one company may not be right for another. Effective organisation structure depends as much as anything on the company culture, where it puts its priorities, its readiness to invest, its status on the digital /multi-channel journey, the impact that digital is having on its customer behaviour and preferences and the size of the digital prize.

In addition, investment in this area will also be driven by the c-Level team. Some teams are inherently conservative and cost conscious, they take an incremental budget /costing /next 12 months approach and will always be reluctant to add to head count unless absolutely essential. Other teams may have more flexibility because their core business is doing well or because they intuitively see the bigger 3 to 5 year picture and recognise that if they don't invest in this area now then shareholder value may start to erode significantly as they potentially struggle to compete in a digital future.

Whatever the right solution for an organisation, then it's also important to stay flexible. Digital is moving and changing as we know fast and unpredictably. No-one was able to forecast the impact of the iPhone or iPad, few today yet understand the impact of digital 3D printing, or how social media is increasingly replacing paid traditional advertising, or how mobile on-the-go connectivity is replacing the desktop and laptop. It's a changing world of course and as companies organise their teams in this area it's important to constantly review the right skills and resources are in the right places!

Chapter 19

Digital evolution of Marketing /Marketing Department organisation structures

1. Background

In the good old days! Marketing was relatively straightforward to organise. Back in the 1970's when the marketing function really began to gain widespread recognition and adoption, there were typically just a few key levers that the department was responsible for. And these were mostly around building brand awareness among the target customer /consumer group.

Today's world however has become infinitely more challenging and complex. The role and responsibility of Marketing has grown significantly. Companies today now almost universally look to their marketing team as their engine of growth. Market sectors are more competitive, they are usually global, they have become multi-channel, technology is proving disruptive while at the same time being attractive, expertise eg in digital, mobile, social, SEO is becoming more specialist and harder to obtain…getting any increase in market share and gains in revenue is just more challenging.

The progressive Marketing function however is now looking to tackle these challenges head-on. They are taking responsibility for developing the company's strategy and plans that can navigate through this market maze and develop winning solutions. The need for an integrated, multi-channel, technically literate, innovative and ever more entrepreneurial team is now becoming paramount.

This chapter looks at the evolution of the Marketing organisation. It starts with "the good old days" and looks at where things now are. There is no "right/proven" structure and model. Every company of course is different. There are differences in B2B and B2C (principally B2B have historically had less "digitally" sophisticated and developed customers, though that is also now rapidly changing!) and companies are very influenced by number of products /number of Brands, number of countries sold to, size of revenue streams, readiness of the senior directors /officers of the company to invest, how responsive the business is to new channels of communication like web, mobile, social, and just how ambitious the marketing team wants to be!

2.The good old days

There were principally two key levers: Promotions and Advertising.

The Proms team developed the annual plan and set out the promotions cycle. They would agree plans with Sales dept. about what sort of incentives required at different stage of the sales cycle. Activity would be driven mostly by the Sales team and the needs of key Trading customers. So there would be something planned for each quarter. The range of options was fairly basic, choose from direct mail, sampling, discounts and if possible eg "on-pack" competitions.

Alongside this and in support would be the *Product /Brand advertising*. This would depend on budgets and would be all about building awareness and recognition. It might be on TV or in Print or on the Radio. (Media buying and planning would invariably be outsourced to the Ad agency)

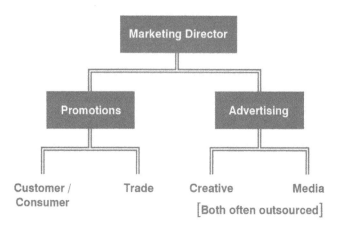

3. The 1990's

Still before the real commercial advent of the internet, yet Marketing even at this point in time was becoming significantly more sophisticated. The catalyst here was the availability of data and more and more computer processing power available on the desktop. Suddenly a marketing team could recruit in a data /insight /research team who could analyse customer behaviour, spot trends, engage in richer and deeper segmentation and identify much more tailored and refined and sophisticated marketing campaigns and activities.

So marketing teams might typically have a Head of Insight (in early days this might have been the Market Research Mgr), who would take responsibility for data and analytics. The work might be outsourced to a specialist data/research team or combined with some in-house expertise.

In addition, the whole concept of the "Brand" began to take root. Brand Mgrs. began to proliferate as companies looked at the pioneer of effective Brand marketing, Procter & Gamble, and wanted to adopt and copy their, it seemed, proven success model. Brand Mgrs. were charged with being the "guardians of the brand". While no-one was quite sure what that meant! it seemed mostly about measuring and monitoring Brand awareness, propensity to purchase and brand sentiment. It also meant being the champion of the brand internally across the company. That usually also meant being the coordinator of brand planning, brand budgets, brand promotions, brand development and brand advertising. And in some instances having those skills reporting directly into them rather than being separated out.

But this era did particularly herald a step-change in the profile and power of Marketing. Marketing Directors began to appear on the main board. The Brand Mgr started to become a powerful figure of influence and responsibility. The team became more than just administrators of a promotions budget. They became responsible formally with Sales for top line revenue growth, and often

took on the Brand/Product P&L. They also had a much more involved role in the long term. No longer just about short term tactical campaigns and quarterly sales programmes. There was now also a key responsibility to use the data and insight to generate product development programmes which would keep the Brand alive and contemporary and compelling.

3. Now!

Today's world has seen a step change in complexity. We now live in this multi-channel, technology-enabled world of innovation, new ideas and constant change. Channels to market have proliferated and fragmented. It's no longer a simple world of TV, Print, Radio. Now add of course so much more whether via desktop, mobile, tablet, webcast, YouTube, Pinterest, Facebook, Twitter, social media monitoring generally, in-game advertising, pre-roll, SEO, SEM, blogs, eCRM, e-Commerce…the list goes on.

And yet, this has all fallen to the Marketing Department. No other team has stood up and tried to take this all on board. And typically no other team in the company would naturally have the skills or market understanding to adopt and embrace all this change and opportunity. So everyone now looks to Marketing. Tell us about these changing market/multi-channel/omni-channel conditions, how do we now reach out to our target audience (they are no longer where they used to be!), get us the data and insight that enables us to understand what marketing communications will work and what will not, conduct the tests that show how to engage with our target customers in this digital world, identify the new programmes and activities and product development which will ensure we remain/become successful!

No small challenge.

And so the Marketing department has had to evolve rapidly. It has had to take on and recruit new skills/ new people. It has had to expand simply to cover the basics. It now is expected to have skills in all these "new" areas and to understand mobile, social, Twitter etc etc. Over the course of the past decade marketing teams have grown in numbers (though not necessarily in comms spending budgets) and have become even more "centre stage". They are now the champions of not just the Brand, but also of the Customer. They now formulate the total customer engagement strategy. Instead of Sales driving Marketing (as used to happen), it's now the other way round. Marketing are the key. They are the ones who are at the heart of the business. It is their knowledge about digital and the changing market environment that is dictating the whole organisation's future strategy. It is now Marketing's relationship with IT that is the core team dynamic. It is how those two departments operate and collaborate and work effectively together that will ultimately decide who will be the winners by 2020.

So in the next two diagrams /org structures, the first illustration shows how the Marketing skills set has proliferated and the range of new skills and functions the team had to adopt. The second chart next page shows how the better Marketing departments have come to terms with this, how they have reorganised to manage that proliferation to find a new simpler more streamlined more manageable and more effective org.solution.

As mentioned at the beginning of this chapter, there are no "right answers". And this has simply tried to show how things have changed, and by just how much! And what some possible ways of navigating the organisation through this changing dynamic period might look like.

(i) Extended Marketing value chain /org.:

(ii) a Streamlined /consolidated /multi-channel Marketing organisation structure:

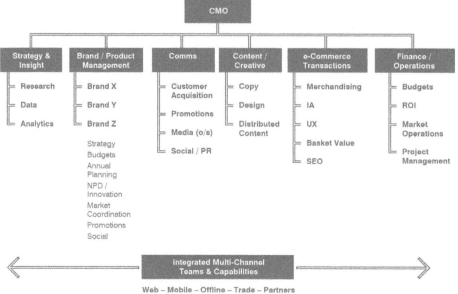

Chapter 20

A market perspective on Digital leadership roles

More than 30% of the Fortune 500 have appointed a senior Digital Leader, often with the title of Chief Digital Officer. And in the past few years the number of such appointments has risen dramatically.

PWC research has shown that there is now wide awareness of digital tools and technologies and "getting digital right" is seen as a potential key engine of future revenue and profit growth. Most of these Digital leadership appointments have been in industry sectors which are consumer-facing

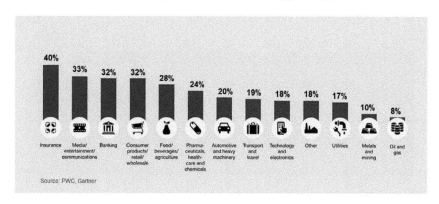

Consumer-facing industries lead the way appointing a CDO

The research is also showing that most Chief Digital Officers or CDOs come from either a Marketing or Technology background. About a third are technologists who have grown up in IT and likely have a Computer Sciences or equivalent degree. Companies are choosing people with such background where they see core advantage coming from improvement in their IT platform as an enabler of change. It may be that they are not satisfied with their existing CTO or perhaps just frustrated at the complexity and blocks in their current legacy IT systems. So bring in a CDO who is also a Technical leader who can challenge and explore new IT solutions that might help the organisation leapfrog over its current stack. Possible but can be politically complex if the CDO and CTO are in conflict over strategy, budgets and direction.

More commonly we see CDOs coming from a Marketing /Commercial background. They may have been Marketers who gradually assumed control of all digital marketing to become more expert at the whole multi-channel consumer engagement. They may also have taken control of online sales and e-commerce and have developed a very broad area of expertise.

They are often in effect "Digital CEOs" with broad Brand, sales and marketing while also managing a growing and often significant online P&L.

No wonder that those CDOs who have the experience and stature to step-up to this CEO-type challenge are few. There are any number of rising stars, grown-up digital, perhaps 10 years work experience who absolutely get the whole multi-channel opportunity. But such people are not yet C-level execs, they don't have enough experience to take on such high levels of responsibility. They don't have the stakeholder manager skills and political nous. So such people do not make the C-suite yet. But, for the many CDOs who do have the right levels of senior experience, it is still not common for them to be at the senior ExCo /leadership /main Board level. They may find they do not report to the CEO but perhaps to the CFO or the CMO. And as a result their remit is more limited, their ability to effect change more curtailed and potentially constrained in driving the transformation and growth that they were brought in for.

In fact, we can see that companies have very different views of what they see in the scope and remit of their newly appointed CDO and what they are targeting and hope to achieve.

Given this variety of reasons for choosing a CDO, it is not surprising to find there are a number of different "typical" CDO remits:

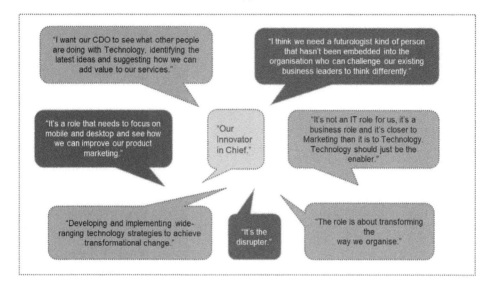

Different types of CDO

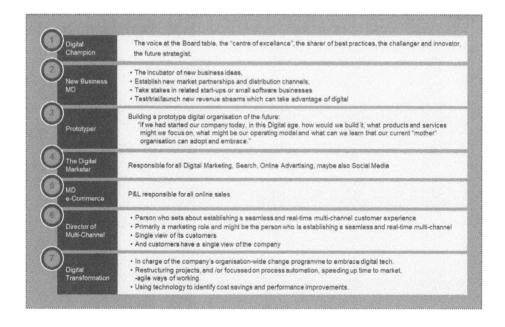

All this CDO challenge and opportunity can perhaps best be captured and summarised in this interview here with Francis Gonczi when Global Digital Leader at EDF Energy:

> *"In appointing me, the company had several goals:*
>
> *(i)   To get closer to customers through digital experiences and data analysis*
> *(ii) To rethink and restructure internal operations and*
> *(iii) To devise disruptive new business models that would generate value.*
>
> *These goals represented a major challenge for a traditional company like ours in a risk-adverse industry. Every small digitalisation project has required everyone around the table to be aligned and agreed. As CDO my role is to serve as the overarching organiser and orchestrator and go-to expert of our digital activities and to ensure a balance of empowering teams, providing oversight, reporting progress and ensuring that things stay on track."*

Chapter 21

Digital eco-systems and incubators

A Gartner survey has found that more than half of the top global 1000 are actively developing and investing in digital eco-systems. A typical example comes from Huawei, the Chinese Networking and Telecoms multi-national, and their commitment to investing and building out their eco-system as another means to secure competitive advantage.

> "With a view to building a digital ecosystem in the Southeast Asia region, Huawei has made an $81 million investment with the theme "Innovate for a Digital Asia-Pacific." Over the next three years, Huawei will invest in setting up open labs, enabling cloud developers, and cultivating ICT talent in the Southeast Asian countries. Huawei's Region President James Wu has unveiled its "developer enablement plan, saying that it's aimed at supporting digital economy growth and cultivating an ecosystem in the region.
>
> "We want to empower developers and promote young talent in Southeast Asia. We have over 30 years of experience and capabilities in the ICT sector. Through APIs and development platforms, we will open up our capabilities to our partners in the region…this is a huge opportunity for developers to create targeted solutions to the digitalization of industries and grow their own business. By working together, we can dream bigger and fly higher."

*****

Before exploring this area further, it's worth just recapping what is a "digital eco-system"? It's been best defined as a "distributed, adaptive, open socio-technical system with properties of self-organisation, scalability and sustainability".

Gartner's take on this is to define it in this way: "a digital ecosystem is an interdependent group of enterprises, people and/or things that share standardised digital platforms for a mutually beneficial purpose, such as commercial gain, innovation or common interest. Digital ecosystems enable you to interact with customers, partners, adjacent industries – and even your competition"

Let's consider some examples:

Danske Bank

- Established a network of partners to create an online Utilities portal
- Aggregator of real time data feeds from realtors, utility and service providers
- Type in post code number of bedrooms in the house or square metres
- Get an estimate of running costs, local taxes, utilities etc.-provide better financing advice, customer support and service
- Become the first stop on a house search

Home Depot

- Launched the Wink connected home network
- "Wink is the quick and simple way to connect you and your home. Manage hundreds of smart products from the best brands in one simple app"
- "Wink allows smart products from different brands (e.g. providing lighting, heating, phone, computing, TV services) to speak the same wireless language so you can easily control them via the Wink app".
- Home Depot has established partnerships with many of its suppliers to create this connected home ecosystem

Philips Healthcare

- Team up with Salesforce.com to build a future health care platform
- An ecosystem of developers building healthcare applications
- Enable collaboration and unified workflow between doctors and patients

- Partnerships with self-care providers, prevention regimes, diagnostics and treatment
- All revolving and tied into a Philips eco-world

Fiat

- Partnering with TomTom, Facebook, Reuters, TuneIn and others to create a Uconnect platform
- To provide drivers with real time news, communication, entertainment, navigation
- Looking in the future to be a one-stop portal for all driver needs from insurance to car servicing

Eco-systems are being seen as a powerful new means to drive business growth and development. It's been described as a "re-imagining of industry and sector boundaries."

"The ongoing digital revolution is reshaping customer expectations...digital pioneers are extending the value proposition...asking what new customer opportunities exist across traditional boundaries...can we leverage partnerships and connections to find new revenues? Greater digital collaboration between G20 companies and entrepreneurs could result in an additional $1.5 trillion in global GDP, an uplift of 2.2 percent, with the top 20 percent of companies committed to collaboration achieving higher levels of revenue growth."

-McKinsey

"Technology is the key and driving solo is no longer an option"

-Jeff Bezos

"Companies that draw 50 percent or more of their revenue from digital ecosystems saw growth and profits 27 to 32 percent higher than average.

-MIT Sloan Management

"Twenty years ago we were building small software systems that may have done one thing and operated in isolation. Now you have platform as a service, infrastructure as a service, security as a service, and all of these systems are starting to integrate.."

-Wired magazine review

"87% of large companies say that open and shared innovation networks will be critical to achieve higher levels of future business performance."

-Accenture survey

In terms of building a successful eco-system, further research from Gartner and from Accenture have helped identify the 6 key components that need to be in place:

1. **API-enabled**: application programming interfaces as the enablers of faster, easier, seamless collaboration and integration
2. **Analytics**: have a core collaborative AI capability to identify new sources of opportunity
3. **Real-time**: build the networking capability that can operate with real-time data /insight feeds
4. **Interoperability**: use shared and common /open source data standards and communication protocols
5. **Innovation culture**: empower and enable an entrepreneurial culture to game-change and capture new business opportunities
6. **Share the passion**: from the CEO and ExCo through the rest of the eco-system team and partner groups

★★★★★

As companies examine and explore these new alliance and open-system opportunities, so at the same time they are often developing them as new businesses. This is frequently on a stand-alone basis, with their own P&L and management teams. And to encourage more entrepreneurial freedom and empowerment, they are also reaching out to Private Equity to co-fund or alternatively establishing their own incubator style start-up /new venture environments where they might launch several eco-system type initiatives, take stakes rather than acquire, share the risk with entrepreneurs who want to retain some ownership and encourage a whole wave of new initiative-taking.

It can be an exciting area of business development and useful to consider just how much support, investment and activity is going on. Looking at just the key UK-based Digital and Tech business incubators, the London digital new venture scene has experienced a rapid rise in incubator and accelerator programmes in the past few years, much faster than any other European city.

Across the UK, research has identified 205 incubators and 163 accelerators supporting an estimated 3,450 businesses, plus 3,660 new businesses a year. These provide up to c.£100m annually in startup investment, according to Wired and the Business Incubators and Accelerators. By way of example, the top 5 London incubator groups are:

1. Seedcamp

Backed by major venture capitalists, angel investors, and corporate entities, Seedcamp has provided early-stage and micro-seed funding to more than 650 entrepreneurs from over 150 startups within 28 industries. Seedcamp-backed companies have raised over $900m in follow-on funding on a $1b valuation.

2. Startupbootcamp

A global accelerator with 21 programmes in major cities including London, New York, Amsterdam, and many more. Each location focuses on a specific tech vertical such as commerce, finance, food, energy, and transportation. London's Startupbootcamp offers three-month accelerated development programming to early-stage FinTech startups.

3. RocketSpace

RocketSpace supports scale-ups with industry focused expertise. The aim is to provide ongoing strategic development through highly qualified corporate collaborators and partnership opportunities.

4. Techstars

"A global force in Tech" with accelerator programs in software, health, retail, mobility, and more, Techstars has supported 1,024 total companies, raising a combined total of over $3.8b on a $9.9b market cap. Global network of mentors and corporate partners, 3 months of office space, and "perks" worth over $1m.

5. Founders Factory

Founders Factory provides both early and late-stage programming for entrepreneurs. With access to a global network of entrepreneurs and top-tier digital talent, Founders Factory has invested in over 200 businesses across six key technology sectors including media, education, beauty, travel, artificial intelligence, and finance. With backing from Aviva, Guardian Media Group, L'Oréal, and others.

Other incubator groups include:

- Imperial College London Enterprise Lab
- Innovify Ventures
- Entrepreneurs Trust
- The Bakery
- Collider

In addition, a growing number of major corporates now have their own very successful e-Ventures investment programmes building out stakes in a number of related companies. The idea is to learn from these new start-ups, be able to potentially take on their ideas and Tech, and ultimately produce new and innovative products and revenue streams.

Companies such as Unilever, Zurich Insurance Group, Microsoft, Intel, Barclays, News Corp UK, JLAB (John Lewis), Tesco, Virgin and many others are doing this,

One of the best and most successful is Telefonica /O2's WAYRA:

As part of a global innovation network open to partners, Wayra UK commits to the internationalisation and scalability of UK-based start-ups. They have invested in some 38 companies across a range of sectors. They house these companies on the 4th floor of the Telefonica central London head office. Telefonica execs are encouraged to drop-in to see what's going on!

Chapter 22

Industry 4.0

Leading B2B companies are using digital to power sales and profit growth

Over the past few years McKinsey has been measuring and evaluating the impact and potential that Digital can have for B2B companies. Digital has been a main preoccupation for B2C companies for a number of years, but B2B companies are now also waking up to the opportunities Digital can bring.

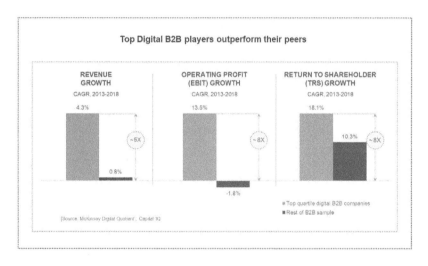

Part of the McKinsey survey has been to assess how ready a company is for Digital Transformation and how developed are its skills and systems to take advantage. There are a number of successful B2B companies who have developed strong Digital capabilities. Organisations like Cisco, Boeing, Wolverine, Ford, Caterpillar, Texas Instruments and others. But most lag the B2C average and closing that gap is going to be crucial. Top-quartile Digital performers grow more sales, earn more profits, and deliver more value to shareholders than the rest of the B2B field.

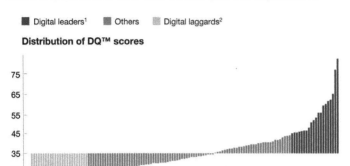

B2B companies trail their B2C counterparts in digitization.

■ Digital leaders[1]   ■ Others   ▨ Digital laggards[2]

Distribution of DQ™ scores

DQ™ score is calculated on a scale of 0 to 100 as the average score of the 4
equally weighted dimensions: Culture, Strategy, Capabilities and Organization.

[1]Digital leaders are defined as companies with a DQ score equal to or above 50.
[2]Digital laggards are defined as companies with a DQ score below 25.

Some of this is not a complete surprise, of course, since the digital ecosystem can be tougher to establish and navigate for B2B companies. Their sales forces face, for example, a far more complex purchasing environment, with multiyear deal cycles in some cases, lengthy RFP processes, and the involvement of many vendors, decision makers, and influencers.

While these complexities are significant, it would be a mistake to use them as an excuse for falling short in some key areas. Digitisation has made consistent, high-quality customer interactions a competitive differentiator. Right now, however, selling models remain largely hitched to offline channels. It's hard for business buyers to get the pertinent and personalised information they need and want from supplier websites and social platforms and harder still to buy directly (though often that is a supplier's intentional strategy).

In addition, while B2B sales teams are working harder to close deals that often involve multiple rounds and many more decision makers, they often lack the real-time analytics and digital tools they need to manage the sale profitably by knowing whom to court with what offer or when to conduct personal outreach.

Incremental changes or pilot efforts can provide benefits, but they aren't likely to significantly close the gap.

Leading B2B companies however do embrace an "all in" digital strategy, knowing it's crucial for making needed core changes. And they don't focus on just digitising sales and customer interactions, but on harnessing digital assets internally to enable their teams to perform better. "Industry 4.0" has become a byword for a full-on review of how digital tools and solutions can unlock significant performance gains across the whole supply chain through automation, real-time connectivity and data and predictive maintenance.

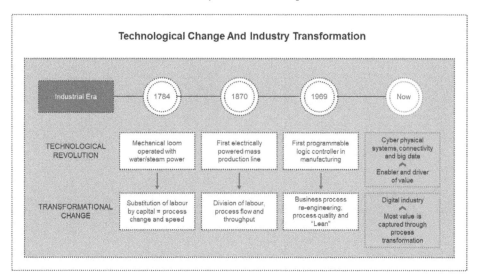

PWC found that Industrial leaders are planning to commit up to $1trillion to Industry 4.0 –around 5% of revenue p.a. A major focus of these investments will be on digital technologies like sensors or connectivity devices, and on software and applications like manufacturing execution systems.

Companies like Ford, Caterpillar, Wolverine, Cisco, Siemens, Bayer, Samsung and others are committing to digital transformation because customers are demanding it, competitive pressures are forcing it and they realise that driving through these changes can uncover new sources of profit and revenue growth. They are also very aware of these sort of market findings:

-   81% of Purchasing/ Procurement Managers said they would choose a supplier that offers an online ordering option over an equal supplier who does not. The reasons were: (i) do business at our convenience, (ii) save time, and (iii) easily monitor order status

-Hybris

-   B2B 2-commerce in the US alone is set to reach $9 trillion in 2019 including through business networks and EDI as well as suppliers' e-commerce sites.

-Forrester report

-   25% of B2B companies in a recent Oracle survey said they now sold direct using e-commerce and 80% of companies in that survey said that they are now actively reviewing this opportunity, whether to launch or invest further

-Oracle

- 68% of companies said that mobile has become a key catalyst and had changed the way distributors and customers wanted to connect and trade

-Forrester /JP Morgan report

- 50% of total sales are predicted through e-commerce by B2B companies. A number are claiming average growth rates of up to 30% +

-Forrester /JP Morgan report

★★★★★

The main area of digitisation is in the Supply Chain, and companies are finding that data and data analytics can be a rich source of innovation. They are especially finding that if they establish an effective eco-system with suppliers and partners and with customers, that they can now take an integrated and complete end-to-end view of parts, process, inventory and distribution, drive hard to a truly just-in-time solution that can provide a win-win-win for all parties and a major reason for partners and suppliers, and also customers, to sign-up, participate and integrate.

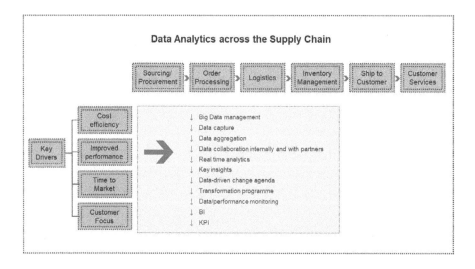

Data and data analytics have a key part to play in identifying opportunities and Machine Learning will ramp up innovation opportunities and ideas and raise the bar on what is possible.

Ford, for example, has used its plant in Cologne, Germany as a key hub for eco-system and "industry 4.0" innovation and change. The plant manufactures 6 types of engine transmission and also supplies Mazda and Volvo across Europe. Total volumes are more than 1 million transmissions each year and there are a significant number of custom variations. The production process involves many different parts from multiple suppliers located in different countries. All this had created an environment where inventory was high and there were frequent delays due to non-availability of parts and the production process was slower than target.

Ford has now introduced its "Material Flows Wireless Parts". This is a wireless messaging infrastructure of 220 RFID (radio frequency identification) tags installed as "Where Call" buttons. Each tag is associated with a specific parts number. A core wifi network has been set up throughout the plant, mobile PCs are mounted at key stages on the production and assembly lines and also at staging points in the warehouse and on the fork lift trucks. Press the "where call" button and the "parts needed" message is immediately directed to the key warehouse area for that part. The supplier is also automatically notified so they can keep track of inventory. They are now responsible for just in time availability and accountable for any failure. As a result of this the assembly line worker stays on station and is trained when to call for replenishment to maintain continuous production. "It's intelligent automation". Ford are now developing AI techniques that could potentially step-change even this "where call" process and develop the predictive modelling that will automatically identify the replenishment timing. So far this initiative has had a 20% improvement in productivity, reduced on-hand inventory to 24 hours, led to a near elimination of down-time and helped forge more effective partnerships with suppliers who now have the visibility and can take more initiative their end as well to improve total supply chain efficiency.

While many manufacturers today are developing and implementing similar real-time inventory management initiatives, others are also looking beyond the production process and at how best to engage the customer to ensure growing demand. One leading example is Cisco. They have been at the forefront in adopting lessons from the B2C environment and enabling their customers to buy anytime anywhere anyhow, a true multi-channel capability.

Cisco are now seen as a leading edge B2B case study in this regard and their journey down this path was kick-started some years ago. This extract below from an interview with Blake Salle, the then Cisco SVP Sales:

"We were doing our annual review and we had one customer who had never purchased from Cisco before and who placed an order online for nearly $100m. The immediate reaction was "hey, where did that come from!" and then our second reaction was: "let's get the Sales team down there straight away". But you know what, when we got in touch, they said ok, no need for your Sales people to visit, just make it easy for us to buy from you.

"What we didn't realise in the early days is also just how important it was to appeal to all online customers big and small. Then we saw buyers from small customers naturally joining the larger companies and buyers still at smaller companies suddenly and dramatically increasing their online order size. And of course it's a small world and word of mouth is strong. So if we'd not dealt with them properly when they were small they sure as anything weren't going to deal with us when they got big."

Cisco: how to buy...it's a main navigation tool on their website:

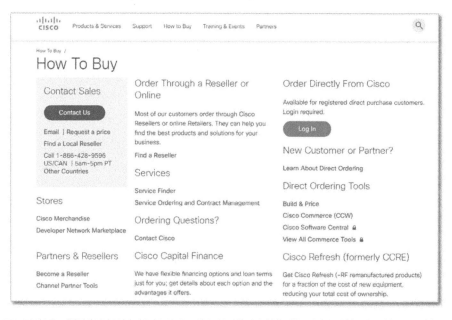

Blake Salle was at the forefront in pushing Cisco into multi-channel selling and still today the Cisco web site is the most B2B sales /buyer friendly and helpful. The main online navigation has *at the top level* a key tab: "How to Buy"

and every option is then laid out: call us, click here for our distribution centres and stores, buy through our partners, here's a list of our resellers and order directly from them, or buy directly online from us, and by the way here's the Cisco App for product specific info and phone numbers for local support near you.

This is a customer /buyer capability which seems so right to set-up and establish but still so many B2B organisations are slow to embrace and implement these sort of initiatives, still relying on the traditional Sales visit to take orders, part implementing new production techniques, still slow to develop open systems and real-time automation in the supply chain, still hesitating about new technology opportunities. It is of course a significant investment to do these things but critical if at all feasible to have the vision and plan and find ways bit by bit to get there, especially if, as Cisco and others are finding, it can open up new sources and ways to drive revenue growth, improve efficiency and cost of delivery and so provide an attractive return and gain.

Chapter 23

Digital IQ

Organisation readiness to drive transformation and change

McKinsey and PWC have been pioneering the idea of Digital IQ, measuring a company's awareness and knowledge around Digital change and most critically an organisation's *readiness* to embrace and implement digital and data transformation.

This IQ index has been developed to help companies determine how ambitious should their change programmes be, how likely it is that they might succeed, what might be the most realistic timetable to set and expect for delivery and what training and support needs might be required to help the organisation and its workforce achieve the kind of changes that are being targeted.

So this IQ index is a crucial audit, an excellent and necessary reality-check. It can be conducted internally by eg the HR team or an outside independent consultancy who can report perhaps most objectively on the possible challenges and blocks that need to be managed and overcome. Transformation is an easy word to say but of course can be very difficult to implement with great success and as we read elsewhere in this book, sadly most transformation programmes do fail. So it can be vital to have this kind of "IQ" check right at the start to potentially provide a blueprint for moving forwards.

McKinsey have carried out a series of Digital IQ surveys and client checks globally especially over the past few years. They are able to show the state of an organisation's ability to cope with large scale change and how that ability compares with eg others in the sector and with the wider business community. If an organisation is shown to be one of the "laggards" then it can be the necessary wake-up call that will indicate the amount of preparation and support required if any major change programme is to be successfully implemented.

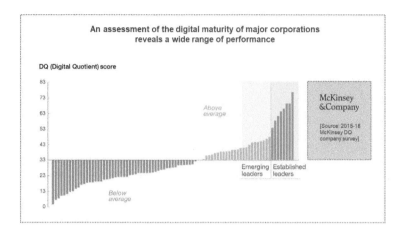

The criteria that are employed in this audit are relatively simple and straightforward but the evidence collected and the benchmarking against others can be very revealing.

Digital IQ

Key tests:
1. *Vison and commitment clearly set-out*
2. *Alignment around the Executive team (that this is a priority)*
3. *Readiness to invest*
4. *Financial stability to carry the costs of transformation*
5. *Right skills and talent*
6. *Resources available*
7. *Culture /people ready*
8. *Analytics in place to measure /monitor*
9. *Data platforms in good state*
10. *Agile methodologies established*

At the most basic level, the IQ audit can evaluate these criteria, and in the context of what are the best practices and benchmarks, then score and rate an individual company. These scores can be a simple score out of 10 with a max

IQ of 100. Any score less that 50 would indicate the organisation is not ready yet for any large-scale transformation and that significant preparatory work is required to enable the company to deliver. A score between 50 and 65 suggests proceed, but with caution, map out the roadmap carefully, pick some of the easiest projects to start with and meantime, work to start filling in the IQ gaps. A score north of 70 would be regarded as positive and an encouraging sign to move ahead, while still being mindful of where there might be needs in the organisation for additional help and support.

This IQ audit is just a guide. It's not intended to be by itself the go /no-go decision-maker. Some companies may be in distress and have little choice about delay and need to get on as best they can. Others will start but perhaps set a longer time-frame to allow the organisation to get up-to-speed and get more confident and comfortable with a transformation agenda. Those who score well will have the knowledge that they can move ahead, set more challenging goals and timetables, still keep an eye on the needs for support and help, but be able to envisage continuing success if they deliver their transformation goals.

Chapter 24

Does investment in Digital pay back?

an introduction to the new "Digital Masters"

Does investment in Digital pay-back? Is it a long term play building a platform for the future that may perhaps deliver 5 years out? Or can investment *now* deliver early wins and results?

There's significant pressure on companies these days to "get digital". This can range from hiring in a new "Chief Digital Officer" to re-launching e-Commerce, expanding social media, setting up advanced Analytics and data mining, automating for self-serve, generating new business leads online, even taking stakes in myriad start-ups…the list of potential opportunities is endless but what's it all worth?

For the first time there's now some reassurance that it *is* all worthwhile. It's not just about doing it because competitors are, or the brokers and analysts expect you to, or because the Marketing and Sales teams are saying you have to, there is now some strong proof and validation that it does truly result in increased profitability to the point of leading sector ROI.

This proof comes from the first truly rigorous piece of research. It was carried out by MIT. Published recently in the Harvard Business Review and also a book called Leading Digital. The top line shows that those who become "Digital Masters" are *26% more profitable* than their industry peers. Those who lag behind in this digital race are 24% less profitable.

It's an extraordinary finding and the research covers some 300 + companies across the world and across different industry sectors. Time and again the MIT team found these high levels of success repeated. So what's going on, what lies behind the research, what's it take to become a "Digital Master"?

To begin with the Research team found there were basically 4 types of companies. These could be categorised as Beginners, "Fashionistas", Conservatives and Digital Masters. And this categorisation was at its most stark when the comparison was done by different industry sector. So it was more likely to find Masters in Retail or Personal Banking. Whereas in B2B Manufacturing, most organisations were well behind the digital curve, despite evidence that even in that sector, those who did invest did get results.

Four levels of digital mastery

Digital Masters outperform their peers

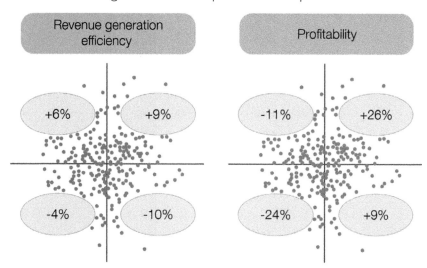

Basket of indicators:
- Revenue/employee
- Fixed-assets turnover

Basket of indicators:
- EBIT margin
- Net profit margin

Digital mastery by industry

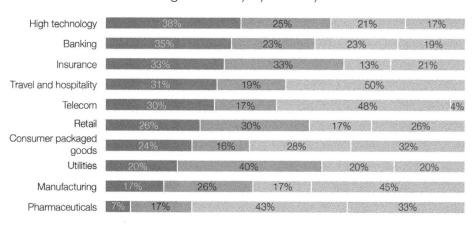

The MIT research has also highlighted what are the key success factors.

While it was for sure about the appetite to invest and the relative amount of investment, it was *also* about the execution and delivery. Some companies were shown to have invested in teams and technology platforms but the investment was kept siloed, the digital team stood on its own, it functioned more as a separate division, there was little integration with the core business, and so little change in the basic business processes and operations. That led to resentment on all sides, frustration in the digital team who were limited in what they could achieve and resentment in the core business who felt much needed investment funds were being diverted.

What led to success was to marry the digital strategy and investment alongside building the digital transformation capability *inside* the core business. The research shows that it was essential to develop the change and implementation leadership skills, to ramp up the PMO team, to identify the core projects and staff them up with leadership and change delivery expertise, that what helped was having a core Steering Committee, led by the CEO, that held weekly or monthly reviews, in-depth, around the change agenda, milestones and progress, so that everyone saw this was a top CEO item and needed the attention and priority to make things happen.

Case Study: Asian Paints is one of these "Digital Masters". They are India's largest paint company and operate across Asia with revenues of c. $2.5bn. Former President and CIO there Manish Choksi attributes their success to "successive waves of digital transformation".

Their aim has been to globalise, maintain high levels of growth (they have hit 15% cagr over past 15 yrs), and to do that while increasing efficiency, innovating and enhancing the customer experience through digital engagement and also important for them, to continue to reduce their environmental impact. "We are spread over 120 locations and deal directly with some thirty thousand retailers so getting our growth strategy right around digital is critical for us".

Among other things they have established a standard e-Commerce platform which all the operating subsidiaries must use, they have one unified and now centralised customer ordering process which is self-serve and online and standardised, the Sales team have embraced this online order process and have changed their role from order-takers to strategic advisors to existing customers while adding a key new business /new customer focus to their work and revenue targets. In addition, steps in the supply chain have been automated with new technology tools and workflow software wherever possible to reduce the level of manpower and error, and they have also taken advantage of new

Cloud-based partner software to better manage relationships. There is now a more in-depth data and performance management capability and that has led to more insight around product profitability and led to the roll-out of a new premium product range to meet a new identified customer segment need. All-in-all a significant set of steps and as Manish Choksi acknowledges: "the road ahead still continues and with our ongoing digital transformation well into the future".

★★★★★

To summarise: the MIT Research team distilled what they found as the 4 key practices which marked out companies like Asian Paints, Unilever, Procter & Gamble, Seven Eleven Japan, EMC, Codelco, American Express, Burberry and a host of others as "Digital Masters". Those 4 key steps are:

1. *"Framing the digital challenge":* A unified consolidated CEO and Board decision that Digital is key to the company's future and the identification of the digital vision, targets and future state.
2. *"Focussing the investment"*: Putting in place the funding for the transformation
3. *"Mobilising the organisation"*: Communicating constantly, reinforcing the same set of messages and goals, using Social Media tools to encourage bottom-up ideation, sharing the rewards and upside as progress gets made.
4. *"Sustaining the transition"*: recognising this is not a one-off exercise, but the need to build a sustainable innovation and change culture, a culture that rewards change and does not condemn well-intentioned failure, an ability to measure progress both internally and externally vs. competition and ensuring a continuous programme of employee awareness-building, education and technical literacy.

★★★★★

The digital transformation compass

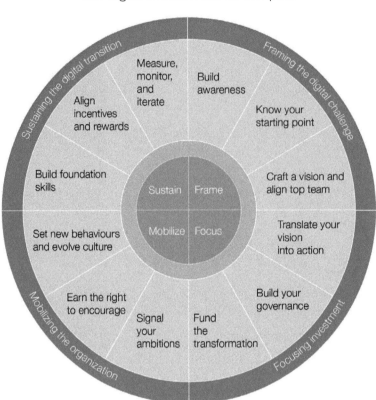

Becoming a "Digital Master" or put another way, leading a successful digital transformation of the company, was rated the biggest challenge facing all organisations no matter what the industry sector in a recent McKinsey study.

It's being able to reach beyond the short term earnings and profits targets and seeing the future 5 year picture and market state, it's being able to see what needs to change, about setting priorities and perhaps most critically somehow finding the funding and investment to enable the change and transformation to take place. At some companies, there is no choice, it becomes a do or die move that can help galvanise the workforce and manage investor expectations of when they can expect a return. But where there's no crisis, as at Asian Paints, it required the Board and CEO to make a fundamental decision about how to succeed in the long term, a reappraisal of strategy, a review of all budget spend, a refocus of effort and activity, a stop on things that weren't clearly about a digital future, a readiness to leverage the balance sheet if necessary, a willingness to consider radical alliances or joint ventures, a desire to "test trial learn".

In the MIT research they suggest this first step for any organisation considering this major change: carry out an internal and confidential survey across the entire workforce and ask this question: "how ready are we to succeed in the digital technology age?" The Digital IQ audit in the previous chapter provides a methodology from McKinsey and PWC on how to best go about that.

Chapter 25

"Courage to Care"

A final thought /observation about the *"courage to care"*.

I was inspired by a lecture given by Joe Garner, the CEO of Nationwide Building Society. Nationwide is a UK Bank with 15 million "members" or customers. They have been consistently voted as one of the best large companies to work for and have won numerous customer care and customer service awards.

When asked about how Nationwide achieves its high levels of employee commitment and engagement, Joe talked about building a culture and spirit which has "the courage to care"

I find it's an inspiring idea which often gets lost in the noise and with all the other demands, priorities and messages that companies have to manage.

Here however are 3 companies that also try to adopt and embrace this.

1. Beiersdorf

Core Values

"Our four Core Values have shaped our corporate culture since the very beginning and are still relevant today. They act as our guiding light and ensure that we speak one language across Beiersdorf. Moreover, they provide us with an orientation for our daily behaviour and serve as a benchmark, we can measure ourselves against."

- **Care** – We act responsibly towards our colleagues, consumers, brands, our society and our environment.
- **Simplicity** – We strive for clarity and consistency, make decisions quickly and pragmatically and focus on what's essential.
- **Courage** – We are committed to bold objectives, take initiative, learn from our mistakes and see change as an opportunity.
- **Trust** – We say what we mean, keep our promises and treat others with respect.

2. Merck

Merck Values – the Foundation of Our Success

"Our company values are the yardstick for our thinking and actions. They are the essence of what ties us together today and tomorrow.

"At Merck, we do business on the basis of common values. Our success is based on courage, achievement, responsibility, respect, integrity, and transparency. These values determine our actions in our daily dealing with customers and business partners as well as in our teamwork and our collaboration with each other."

Courage Achievement Responsibility Respect Integrity Transparency

Courage opens the door to the future.

- Courage requires trust in one's own abilities.
- Courage leads to a healthy self-perception.
- Courage supports the competence needed to execute decisions in change processes.

- Courage means: We challenge ourselves.
- Courage opens us to new ideas

Responsibility determines our entrepreneurial actions.

- Responsibility characterizes our behaviour towards customers, employees, investors and service providers.
- Responsibility means treating our natural resources with care and vigilantly protecting our environment.
- Responsibility determines our business decisions, which we jointly endorse.
- Responsibility means setting a good example.
- Responsibility leads to recognition and acceptance of our business activities.

3. Iggesund Holmen Group

Core values
- "The Group's strategic HR vision is that Iggesund Holmen shall be a company distinguished by employees who, with courage, commitment and responsibility, perform at their best. Also, we believe that when our people are involved in and proud of their company, they are engaged in their personal continued development and the success of everyone here."
- Holmen's shared values are courage, commitment and responsibility.

Courage
- "Courage to act. Holmen's employees are action oriented and make decisions that lead to tangible results. The company rewards innovative thinking that leads to improvements and solves challenges. The Group believes in transparency internally within the company and with the surrounding community.

Responsibility
- Responsibility based on sensitivity and skills. Holmen's employees create participation by involving each other, sharing ideas and providing opportunities to exercise influence. Holmen takes action at an early stage and demonstrates drive when tackling challenges from the environment in which we operate and is proactive about improvement. Holmen's employees are professional in the way in which we run and develop

our operations and we foster sustainable relationships with customers, stakeholders, colleagues and the surrounding community.

★★★★★

Jeffrey Pfeffer, the Harvard Professor, has written and lectured for a long time about building and encouraging the workforce to care and how companies can build "advantage through people".

His take is that: "sustainable competitive advantage has proved elusive for companies. While making enormous investments in technology, research, and state-of-the-art marketing, many of today's managers continue to ignore the single most important factor in achieving and maintaining competitive success: people. Yet all evidence indicates that the source of competitive advantage, in this age of demanding digital and data transformation, may rest more and more on how a company manages and cares for its employees."